Gemstone
DETECTIVE

Buying Gemstones and Jewellery
WORLDWIDE

First Edition

18/3/2024

Kim Rix GG (GIA)

Published by
Filament Publishing Ltd
16, Croydon Road, Waddon, Croydon,
Surrey, CR0 4PA, United Kingdom
Telephone +44 (0)20 8688 2598
Fax +44 (0)20 7183 7186
info@filamentpublishing.com
www.filamentpublishing.com

© Kim Rix 2019

The right of Kim Rix to be identified as the author of this work
has been asserted by her in accordance with the
Designs and Copyright Act 1988.

ISBN 978-1-912635-46-7

Printed by Akcent Media

I've had the pleasure of knowing Kim for over seven years. Our relationship began when I commissioned her to take photos of my grandchild, for an album to commemorate his treasured first year. Her expertise and skill behind the camera are exemplary and she captured our grandson's beauty and character perfectly. She has just finished the same for my delightful granddaughter and I wouldn't want anyone else taking professional photos of our family.

Kim has become a close friend and I've followed with interest her journey as a gemmologist and author. It's no surprise that she's approached this venture with the same passion and professionalism as her photography business. Her guidebooks will be invaluable to travellers wishing to purchase precious gems, even inspiring those who may not have had an interest before.

With over forty years in the financial services industry, I help my clients increase income and grow capital by sharing innovative ways of investing worldwide. My business philosophy is in line with this book, as the intention to share knowledge, experience and contacts (ensuring people have the tools to make the right decisions and safeguard their money, whether it's buying a property or a gem) is the same and I can relate to it wholeheartedly.

Lesley Reeves
SLR Wealth Services Limited

Australian black opal © Kim Rix

Kim Rix GG (GIA)

Contents

Tourists are welcomed at the jewellery factory, Chanthaburi, Thailand © *Kim Rix*

Kim Rix GG (GIA)

What a poser! Antipaxos, Greece © Kim Rix

Kim Rix GG (GIA)

INTRODUCTION

Gemstone mining in Sri Lanka © Kim Rix

Kim Rix GG (GIA)

Why you need this book

If you have bought this book, perhaps you are planning a holiday to some far-flung exotic location and are hoping to bring back a souvenir. Perhaps you are already strolling round the shopping streets and markets, enticed by the beautiful gemstones on offer, but not knowing where to start. Whatever your situation, this book will give you the information you need to make an informed and confident purchase.

I have travelled to over fifty countries in my lifetime. With 196 countries in the world, that's only just over a quarter, so I'm looking forward to adding many more countries and memories to my list during the course of writing this book series.

In the last twelve years, every holiday I've taken has represented an opportunity to explore the gemstones of that country and bring back a keepsake. I've bought rubies from Thailand, pearls in Mauritius, amethyst from Greece, moonstone from Sri Lanka, gold from Dubai and, most memorable of all, I found myself sporting a gorgeous diamond when my husband proposed to me in the Bahamas!

Whether you're shopping for the perfect ring to slip onto your loved one's hand or a present for your best friend, you'll certainly be looking for some reliable advice on what to buy... and what to avoid. As a tourist, you are vulnerable – there are a lot of dodgy geezers out there. Dishonest people can use your lack of local knowledge to get you to part with your hard-earned cash, and there are unfortunately many well-worn gem scams across the world. That's where *Buying Gemstones & Jewellery Worldwide* comes in.

This book is about buying gemstones wherever you are in the world. You will find all the information you need to buy a gemstone or piece of jewellery with confidence. Don't worry if you have little or no knowledge about gemstones — I have written this book with you in mind. Read it before you buy and you'll save a lot of time and heartache.

The internet is a confusing place. It's very hard to find everything you really need to know — all the tips and tricks to help you avoid the pitfalls. Designed to fit in a pocket or handbag, my book will give you the information you need in an easy-to-read format.

This book is not about buying discount gems. However, it will help you to make an informed decision about what and where to buy. It will give you the knowledge needed to feel comfortable that your purchase is genuine and therefore make the whole experience fun and memorable for the right reasons.

Much more than that, though, I want you to enjoy the fun, romance and sense of accomplishment in finding and buying your perfect gem abroad. What an incredible way to remember your special holiday!

Tasty beach hospitality near Cancun, Mexico © Kim Rix

Kim Rix GG (GIA)

What makes me an expert?

I have travelled across the world and spent years honing my knowledge to share this information with you. I've acquired a few gemstones along the way and take every opportunity to expand my local knowledge, along with my collection. Everything in this book is based on personal experience.

The letters after my name are testament to my knowledge. I'm a gemmologist, qualified by the GIA (Gemological Institute of America) — the world's leading authority on gemstones. However, it's my extensive global travel and research that will make this book so useful to you.

My list of colleagues, friends, and genuinely reliable contacts around the world is now large enough to enable me to get in amongst the hustle and bustle of the global gem trading community, to bring you the best tips for buying in many different countries.

I also hope that writing this book will ultimately benefit the jewellery trade around the world. I am a great believer in giving back! I'm just so very lucky to be able to combine my three passions for a living, and giving back is a way for me to express my gratitude. I want my book to help you find your perfect gem at the right price. I also sincerely hope that it helps to boost the small gem-trading businesses: the exceptionally hard-working miners, dealers and jewellers who, like all of us, are trying to make a living in challenging times.

Untreated sapphire, rutile silk 'needles' © E.Billie Hughes/Lotus Gemology

Kim Rix GG (GIA)

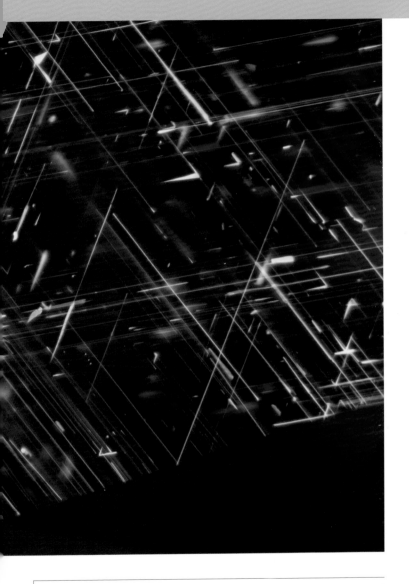

Wonderful cocktails in Cancun, Mexico © Kim Rix

Kim Rix GG (GIA)

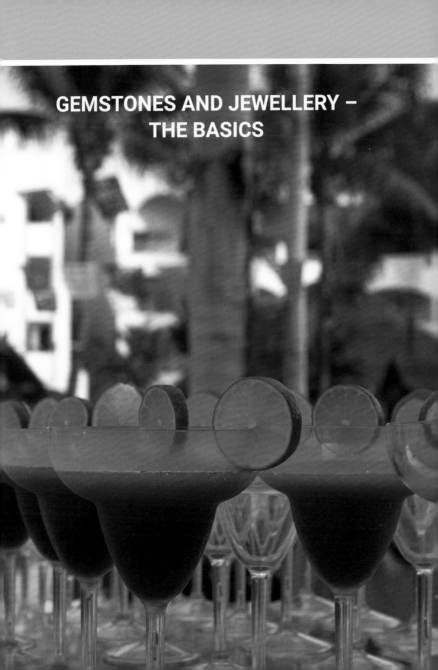

GEMSTONES AND JEWELLERY – THE BASICS

Deciding what you want

There are a few questions you need to ask yourself before purchasing:

Cut stone or rough?
In many countries you will be able to have a rough stone beautifully cut and set within hours. Seeing your gemstone transformed from its rough state to a finished piece of jewellery can give it even more sentimental value. But note that not all countries will let you export rough!

What's the stone for?
For what purpose are you buying a gemstone? Is it for a ring, a brooch, a bracelet, a necklace? How regularly do you intend to wear it? This is where the **durability** of a stone is important, as some stones are too fragile to be worn on the fingers or as a pendant that could get knocked. The **Mohs scale of hardness** is system that grades minerals from softest to hardest on a scale of 1-10. Talc is the softest material at 1, whereas diamond is the hardest at 10. A mineral can only be scratched by a mineral equal or harder than it on the Mohs scale. See page 135 for more information on durability. Depending on the look you are after, you will also need to consider the size and cut of the stone. Another approach is simply to buy a gem that speaks to you and have the setting made to suit that gem.

How much do I want to spend?
This is important. You need to decide on a budget before you approach anywhere that sells gemstones. Arm yourself with a ceiling figure before you start or, in the heat of the moment, you may end up spending more than you want or can afford.

How do I want to pay?
How you want to pay will affect where you buy. Most dealers will be pleased to accept cash. Indeed, you may well get a better deal by

paying cash, as card-processing fees are usually added to the overall price of the gem. In some countries, not all dealers will accept credit cards, especially if you buy from the market or direct from the miner. On the other hand, paying by credit card affords you a certain level of protection under section 75 of the UK Consumer Credit Act, on purchases between £100 and £30,000.

Where do I want to do my gemstone shopping?
Knowing your budget and how you want to pay should determine where you should buy: in a luxury hotel, at a large and established jewellery shop, at a jewellery show, in a museum, at a small gemstone merchant/trader, at the gemstone market...

Gem market, Chantaburi, Thailand © Kim Rix

Kim Rix GG (GIA)

Knowing what you're looking at

Taste is a very personal thing. You may fall in love with a gem that is not particularly valuable, and that's just fine – enjoy it! What you want to avoid is paying more than the gem is worth, and that's when a little knowledge comes in very handy.

A good rule of thumb when buying a gem is to remember the **Four Cs: colour, clarity, cut** and **carat weight**. When it comes to buying most gemstones, however, you also need to factor in origin and treatment. Let's take these one by one.

Colour

Colour is the most important factor in the price of a gemstone. It's not as simple as a gemstone being 'blue' or 'red', though. A gemstone's colour actually incorporates three separate aspects: the saturation, the hue, and the tone.

Saturation

Saturation refers to the amount of colour in the stone. A stone's saturation is the most important factor in its valuation. Stones with low saturation may appear washed out, whereas stones with high saturation may appear too dark. The most valuable stones have medium saturation.

Hue

Hue is a more specific term for colour and refers to the particular shade of the stone's colour. Gemstones are described by their primary (dominant) and secondary hue. In a written description of any gemstone, the primary hue will have a capital letter and the secondary hue will have a lower case letter. For example, you might see a ruby described as 'Red' or 'Red-orange'. Some hues are considered more desirable than others, depending on the gemstone.

Tone

The tone refers to the depth of colour in a stone — how light or dark it appears. A stone that is too light won't show the colour to its best effect, whereas a stone that is too dark will lack brilliance. Make sure that you look at your stone in both artificial and natural light. Cup your hand over it. The stone should appear lively and brilliant, even in shade.

Rutilated quartz, cut by John Dyer. Photography © Priscilla Dyer

Clarity

It's common for many gemstones to have **inclusions** (flaws) when seen under a microscope, so if you are shown a stone that looks flawless under magnification, ask yourself, "Is it too good to be true?". However, the inclusions in a high-quality stone shouldn't be visible to the naked eye. The position of the inclusion also affects the price. A stone with inclusions in the centre will generally be cheaper than an equivalent stone with an inclusion nearer the edge, for obvious aesthetic reasons.

Cut

The quality and type of cut affects the value. When cutting a gemstone, the aim is to retain as much of the weight as possible while achieving the most beautiful effect. It's a fine balancing act! Watch out for areas that don't reflect light and so don't seem to sparkle. These are called **windows** and they detract from the brilliance and value of the stone. A gem with a large face and a shallow bottom will produce this effect.

To check for windowing, place the gem on a piece of paper with text on it and look directly down on it at an angle of 90°. If there is a lighter area in the middle through which you can read the text, the gem has a window. Some sellers will try to overcharge for windowed stones, relying on a tourist's lack of expertise.

I should say here that most stones will demonstrate windowing to some degree when viewed at an angle. What you need to watch out for is windowing that is obvious when viewed directly from above.

Carat

Carats are units of weight in gemstone terminology (1 carat = 200 mg = 0.2g). The higher the carat weight, the heavier and more expensive the gemstone. Price per carat increases at 2, 3 and 4 carats. A 4-carat stone will cost more per carat than a 2-carat stone because of the rarity of larger stones.

Origin

A stone's origin can affect its value as certain locations have become associated with the high quality of the gemstones mined there. Unfortunately, this means that stones are often labelled with a false origin to inflate the price. The only way to determine a stone's origin is to have it tested in a lab. Be aware that the test for origin cannot usually be performed on a stone that has already been set.

Treatment

Your primary aim should be to make sure the gemstone you are about to buy is genuine and not a piece of cheap fakery. Gemstone treatment techniques have become pretty sophisticated and this can work both to the buyer's advantage and against it...

 Remember: be on your guard if someone tries to sell you a good-looking, 'untreated' stone! If it looks too good to be true, it almost certainly is.

Before you buy any gemstone, you should always check its certificate or get it tested for authenticity. You'll find details of how to do this later in the chapter. Do note, though, that many labs will only test a cut and polished stone for authenticity. Buying a rough stone is more of a risk than buying a cut stone.

Kim Rix GG (GIA)

Multi-stone rings, Myanmar (Burma) © Kim Rix

The best-known gemstones

Diamond, emerald, ruby and sapphire are known as 'The Big Four' gemstones because they are the most famous gemstones of all — and subsequently among the most expensive.

Diamond

Though it was the company De Beers who coined the advertising slogan 'A Diamond is Forever' in 1947, diamonds have been known for their exceptional hardness throughout history. Measuring 10 on the Mohs hardness scale, diamonds are the hardest natural substance on earth, making them not only 'a girl's best friend' but also an excellent choice for everyday jewellery like engagement rings.

A solid form of carbon, diamonds are best known in their colourless form, but can also occur in many other shades, including yellow, pink, green, blue and even black. Coloured diamonds are known as fancy diamonds.

Diamond is the birthstone for April and is traditionally associated with strength and clarity.

Emerald

Emerald is what we call the deep green variety of the gemstone beryl (light green is simply referred to as 'green beryl'). Emerald is often presented in a rectangular cut with angled corners — hence the name 'emerald cut'. This cut makes the most of the rich blue-green to pure green of the finest stones. The angled corners add stability and help to prevent damage to the gemstone — emerald is quite brittle, despite being reasonably hard.

Flawless emeralds are extremely rare and extraordinarily expensive. A good quality emerald will have **inclusions**, but these should only be visible under magnification. Inclusions visible to the naked eye will bring down the price. The inclusions in an emerald are moss-like and can be quite beautiful in their own way — the French term for them is 'jardin', which means 'garden.'

Emerald, a symbol of love and compassion, is the birthstone for May. It is also associated with growth and vigour, so would make a wonderful gift for a keen gardener — as long as the jewellery isn't worn while digging the flowerbeds!

Sapphire

Sapphire is a variety of a mineral called corundum. Sapphires occur in many different colours, but not in red: if the corundum is red, we call it a ruby instead. The two gemstones are distinguished by colour alone, as their structure is the same. Corundum is the second-hardest mineral after diamond and has a remarkable ability to withstand scratching. This makes sapphire a practical as well as an aesthetic choice in jewellery pieces for everyday use, especially rings and bracelets.

Though traditionally thought of as deep royal blue, sapphires come in every colour of the rainbow. Australia is famous for its *parti-coloured* stones, which contain two or more colours. Sapphires are valued in much the same way as diamonds, but with more emphasis on colour and carat size, and even the origin of the stone.

Exquisite Burmese ruby jewellery © Kim Rix

Kim Rix GG (GIA)

The birthstone for September, sapphire is associated with wisdom, royalty, good fortune and the heavens and symbolises fidelity when used in an engagement ring. Reiki healers believe that sapphire channels healing powers.

Ruby

Like sapphire, ruby is a variety of corundum. While 'pigeon blood' rubies from Burma are considered the finest in the world, rubies are mined in many other countries. The term pigeon blood refers to the intense red of the ruby, which is said to resemble the first few drops of blood from a freshly killed pigeon. Corundum is an extremely hard mineral, which makes ruby an excellent choice for setting within a frequently worn ring. Don't expect to buy a flawless natural ruby unless you have vast amounts of money to invest — almost all rubies contain inclusions (flaws).

Ruby is the birthstone for July and symbolises love, passion and power. The traditional gift for a 40th wedding anniversary is a ruby and a 40th jubilee is called the Ruby Jubilee. Rubies were once believed to soothe inflammation and older women would rub ground ruby into their skin in the hope that it would restore the bloom of youth. Some alternative therapists maintain that rubies stimulate energy, positivity and sensuality.

Other gemstones

Alexandrite

What makes alexandrite special is the way it appears to change colour. A high-quality alexandrite will seem to be grass green in natural light but rich red under artificial light. This is due to the way in which alexandrite absorbs and reflects various wavelengths of light in different lighting conditions.

By day

The price of an alexandrite will be determined by the hue and the extent of the colour change. The most valuable stones have a very distinct colour change and display as close to true green and true red as possible. If you are torn between an emerald and a ruby, alexandrite may be the gemstone for you!

By night

Amethyst

Amethyst is a purple variety of quartz. It was once considered a precious gem, but was downgraded to semi-precious status after large reserves of it were uncovered in Brazil.

Amethyst is the birthstone for February. In 2018, ultraviolet was named Colour of the Year by Pantone, the colour company. If 2018 was special for you, vivid purple amethyst could be your perfect keepsake.

Aquamarine

Aquamarine — or 'water from the sea' in Latin — is one of several pretty colour varieties of the mineral beryl. Aquamarine, as the name might suggest, is a light blue or bluish green. These variations in colour are caused by the presence of

Kim Rix GG (GIA)

different types of chemical impurity within the makeup of the gemstone. You will probably be familiar with deep green beryl — as mentioned earlier, it's more commonly known as emerald.

As aquamarine is a reasonably durable gemstone, it works well in everyday jewellery. To accentuate the lovely colour of an aquamarine, buy one with a step cut.

Aquamarine is one of the birthstones for March and is credited with all sorts of powers, from calming the sea to soothing a toothache. An aquamarine might also be a good bet if you've forgotten your anniversary — it's said to bring happiness to marriages!

Chrysoprase

Chrysoprase is a variety of chalcedony found mostly in Australia, Africa and Brazil. A fairly durable stone, chrysoprase is suitable for use in most jewellery with the usual caveats if handled with care. The name chrysoprase means 'golden leek' in Greek — it has a fresh, green colour caused by deposits of nickel. Despite its name, yellow tones in chrysoprase are not as desirable as blue-green tones or the true apple-green of a high-quality stone.

Perhaps it is chrysoprase's bright cheerful hue that makes it a traditional cure for depression and anxiety!

Citrine

Citrine is a type of quartz, whose yellow tint is caused by the presence of iron. Occurring in hues ranging from orange and brown to a pale yellow, it's perfect for lovers of sunshine shades. Once thought to be rare, large reserves found in the 20th century mean that citrine has come down hugely in price. This has made it a great choice for striking and bold pieces of jewellery, as it is possible to buy excellent quality stones in large sizes at very reasonable prices.

Citrine's bright yellow and orange radiance has traditionally been associated with healing of both body and mind, and is said to be particularly therapeutic for sufferers of depression.

Garnet

'Garnet' is an umbrella term for a group of closely-related varieties of mineral. It occurs in a range of colours, but most commonly in shades of red. A rare blue-to-pink colour change variety has, in recent years, been unearthed in Madagascar. Warm reddish hessonite is the most commonly occurring garnet, and the orange-coloured spessartite the most expensive.

Garnet is the birthstone for January and the gem for a 2nd wedding anniversary. It is thought to bring luck and keep its wearer safe. Garnet was perhaps not so lucky for those unfortunate to encounter it in battle, though — some armies used to fashion bullets from garnet, believing that its glowing red colour would make wounds deadlier!

Kim Rix GG (GIA)

Some people maintain that square garnets help people succeed in business. A gem for the high-flyer in your life, perhaps?

Iolite

Iolite is commonly known as 'water sapphire' because its colour can be very similar to genuine sapphire. Be aware that the two are very different gemstones! Derived from the Greek word 'ios', meaning 'violet', iolite occurs in shades of purple, blue and grey. Iolite is becoming popular as an affordable alternative to more expensive stones like sapphire and tanzanite. Though reasonably durable, it is still softer than tough sapphire and so should be treated with a little care. No treatment has yet been used successfully on iolite, so you can assume that any particularly fine example will be entirely natural.

Iolite is associated with mind, spirit and imagination. Those who practise alternative forms of therapy use it to ease insomnia and induce dreaming. Some believe that iolite can help those who are disorganised, distracted and lacking in motivation. Parents of difficult teenagers, take note!

Jade

Though we tend to think of jade as a green gemstone, it occurs in many other colours too. The name jade actually refers to two different gemstones — jadeite and nephrite — which until the 19th century were thought to be the same stone. The type prized by ancient Chinese artisans was jadeite because it was denser, more lustrous and easier to carve. Particularly high-quality jadeite was reserved for the Emperor alone and called Imperial Jade. Nephrite jade is more common than jadite and considered less valuable. Slightly softer on the Mohs scale than jadeite, nephrite also has a lower translucency and lustre.

Jade is said to be good for disorders of the kidneys and is used by some to promote mental clarity.

Kunzite
Kunzite was only discovered in 1902 by George Frederick Kunz – you may have heard about his connection with Tiffany's. Like tanzanite, kunzite is **pleochroic**, meaning that its colour appears to change when viewed from different angles. Kunzite comes in pretty shades of pink and violet and, along with many pink stones, is associated with femininity and love.

The perfect gift for a new mother, kunzite is sometimes called 'the woman's stone' because it is said to help distressed or overactive children to sleep well.

Lapis Lazuli
High quality lapis lazuli is prized for its deep blue colour and was particularly loved by the ancient Egyptians. The golden specks that appear in many specimens are pyrite. It makes a good gemstone for bold pieces of jewellery, as it's often found in very large chunks.

A symbol of wisdom and truth, lapis lazuli is associated with royalty.

Kim Rix GG (GIA)

Moonstone

Moonstone is an exquisite semi-precious gemstone that appears to glow from within, thanks to an optical effect called **adularescence**. Varieties of moonstone are found across the globe, and blue moonstone (found only in Sri Lanka) is more expensive than other types, due to its rarity.

Moonstone is traditionally cut in the form of a cabochon — a smooth, unfaceted round, oval or teardrop shape. Moonstone is not very tough, so will need careful handling. It's probably not an ideal gemstone for everyday jewellery likely to get knocked.

Given moonstone's bewitching appearance, it is no surprise that this gem is credited with mystical powers. Some consider moonstone a love charm and others believe that it has the power to foretell the future. It would certainly make a magical present for that special someone!

Morganite

Like emerald, morganite is a type of beryl. Its delicate pink to violet colour comes from manganese inclusions in the crystal structure. Set in rose gold, morganite looks particularly pretty and has a beautiful, vintage appeal.

Because morganite was discovered relatively recently — in 1911 — it has not had time to develop the traditional uses and folk wisdom associated with other gemstones. However, pink gemstones tend to symbolise love, passion and romance.

Opal

No two opals are the same. Finding the right opal is such a personal process that it is often said that the opal chooses you, rather than the other way round!

Opal starts its life as rain. As the water seeps down through the earth, it picks up silicon dioxide from the sandstone through which it passes. This silica solution pools in any cracks and voids in the rock, then evaporates, leaving behind a deposit of silica — the opal. It's the tiny impurities suspended within the silica that produce the opal's individual flashes and patterns of colour.

One of the official birthstones for October, opal has for thousands of years been associated with good fortune, prophecy and protection from harm. Its magical play of colours may equally be the source of some bad-luck lore associated with opal, too — it was once believed to have been a stone used by witches.

Peridot

Peridot, a variety of the mineral olivine, occurs in only one colour: green. The precise hue depends on the amount of iron present in the crystal structure, and can range from a bright, citrusy shade to a deeper, grassier colour.

Peridot occurs all over the world, and is particularly associated with meteor crash sites. Scientists have discovered peridot in mineral samples gathered by space probes near the sun, so peridot is

Kim Rix GG (GIA)

sometimes referred to as the extra-terrestrial gemstone. One for the UFO spotters and Trekkies among you, perhaps?

Its clarity makes peridot a sparkly gem — perfect for parties and occasion jewellery. If you're prone to nightmares, peridot is said to protect the wearer from bad dreams!

Quartz

Quartz, a natural form of silicon dioxide, is the most abundant mineral found on earth. As a gemstone, it comes in every colour under the sun. The most well-known quartz gemstones are amethyst and citrine.

Other varieties of quartz include:

Ametrine — a pretty mixture of two minerals, purple amethyst and yellow citrine. It is also referred to as bolivianite because it's mostly mined in Bolivia.

Aventurine — a type of green quartz, sometimes confused with jade.

Green quartz/prasiolite — this is the green version of amethyst and is considered a collector's item.

Jasper — a microcrystalline variety of quartz.

Rose quartz — a soft blush pink, a stone for attracting love into your life.

Rutilated quartz — contains naturally occurring strands of Rutile.

Smoky quartz – a typically brown, greyish or black. Be on your guard for 'smoky topaz' that's really smoky quartz.

Tourmaline quartz – has needle-like inclusions of black tourmaline.

Spinel

Spinel's relative durability and excellent light refraction make it a popular, less costly, alternative to the traditional Big Four — diamond, ruby, sapphire and emerald. Spinel occurs in a wide range of colours.

Blue spinel is particularly special because it occurs naturally. There are no known treatments for spinel and so, unlike other blue gemstones such as sapphire, tanzanite and aquamarine, you can be sure that your blue spinel is completely unaltered by human hands, other than being cut, polished, etc.. As with sapphire, blue spinel with a high colour saturation and medium tone commands the highest prices.

Tanzanite

In the year 2002, this gemstone joined the Big Four family, making it officially the Big Five. It also made it into the birthstone chart – the first change to the list since 1912. Discovered in 1967 in the hills of Merelani, just below Kilimanjaro in northern Tanzania, it has never been found anywhere else since. Tanzanite comes from the mineral family zoisite and is pleochroic, meaning you'll see different colours if you tilt it in different directions. Along with zircon and turquoise, tanzanite is a birthstone for December, and it's also the gem for a 24th anniversary. Blue tanzanite is more prized than purple or violet.

Topaz

Pure topaz is colourless, but topaz occurs in many different colours, depending on the natural impurities present or the type of treatment it has undergone. Natural topaz tends to be brown-gold, grey or yellow, but treatment will produce more vivid and intense colours, including the most popular topaz colour, blue. A pretty, pinkish-orange colour referred to as 'imperial' topaz is the most valuable natural colour variation as it's rare. Topaz is a reasonably durable gemstone, but will chip or crack if given a hard knock.

Topaz is the birthstone for November and is also somewhat of a gemmological cure-all. When worn as a necklace, topaz was believed to dispel enchantment, bring wisdom and chase away the blues. The ancient Greeks thought it could increase strength on the battlefield, detect poisons and even turn its wearer invisible. Mixed with wine, topaz was considered a cure for burns, haemorrhages, insomnia and respiratory difficulties. If you work in a medical profession, topaz is your gemstone!

Tourmaline

The name 'tourmaline' comes from a Sinhalese phrase 'tura mali', which means 'stone mixed with many colours.' Tourmaline has a huge number of colour variations ranging from blue-green and green to a yellowish brown that looks like rich honey. You can also buy a red variety, which goes by the name rubellite.

Tourmaline is one of October's birthstones and is traditionally used for healing. Some professional athletes claim that tourmaline helps them to recover from intense workouts and it is even believed to boost vitality and vigour in the bedroom!

Turquoise

Prized since antiquity, especially by the Egyptians and Aztecs, Turquoise is an opaque, blue-to-green gemstone, usually cut as a cabochon. Its vivid colour is due to the presence of copper. The most valuable turquoise gemstones have no matrix (the non-precious stone surrounding the veins of turquoise), though the combination of turquoise and matrix can produce a pleasingly striking effect.

Turquoise is one of December's birthstones and is said to be healing, calming and strengthening, particularly when used near the throat chakra. If public speaking scares you, a turquoise necklace might just do the trick!

Zircon

Zircon occurs in a range of colours, of which blue is the most valuable. Colourless zircon can be a cheaper alternative to diamond, due to its excellent lustre and brilliance. Don't confuse the semi-precious gemstone zircon with a synthetic imitation diamond called cubic zirconia, though — they are two separate substances! Zircon is somewhat softer than diamond, so is not ideal for jewellery worn every day. It also tends to darken and grow dull when exposed to regular sunlight.

Zircon is the birthstone for December and has many traditional uses. In the middle ages, Zircon was believed to aid sleep, encourage wealth, and cultivate wisdom and honour. Nowadays, many people trust in Zircon to increase their self-confidence and develop compassion for themselves and others.

© Kim Rix

Some gemstones are not actually gemstones in the true sense of the word. To be classified as a gemstone, it must be beautiful, durable and rare. Though most gemstones are minerals, some develop from a biological process involving animals or vegetables. The most prized of these organic gemstones are pearl, amber, coral, jet and ammolite. The sale of ivory and tortoiseshell is now banned or strictly regulated in many countries.

Amber
Amber is the fossilized resin of long-extinct trees, dating back approximately 320 million years. Deposits of amber can be found all over the world, though the best-known amber is Baltic amber from the coast of the Baltic Sea. It occurs in different colours, the most common being yellow, followed by green. Rarer colours include red and blue. Amber may be heated or dyed to enhance the appearance and colour of the stone. Certain inclusions are considered desirable and this is because the inclusions are often of great interest — an amber pendant may contain, for example, a fossilized prehistoric insect or plant.

Amber is used by many people for its purported pain-relieving properties. It's common practice in many countries to use an amber necklace or bracelet to soothe a teething baby. Of course, anything that goes around a baby's neck should be used with extreme caution!

Ammolite
Good quality ammolite is stunningly beautiful and, very much like opal, gives wonderful flashes of colour. Formed from the fossilized shells of

ammonites, ammolite is as old as the dinosaurs. Gem-quality ammolite is extremely rare and mostly found in Canada.

Coral

Like the bones in our body and pearls, coral is made of calcium carbonate. It's formed from the skeleton-like structures of underwater organisms called coral polyps, which are harvested and polished to produce beads, cabochons and irregular-shaped branches for use in jewellery. Red, or 'precious,' coral is deep red to pink in colour, and was traditionally harvested in the Mediterranean. Much of the coral used by Mediterranean jewellers is now imported from elsewhere due to dwindling stocks (see page 74, under 'The ethics of buying gemstones').

It is important to note that the export of certain types of coral is illegal in many countries. Always do your research and check that your purchase is above board.

Jet

Jet is a black gemstone derived, like coal, from fossilized wood. Cut and polished, it makes very striking jewellery. The most important sources of this lightweight gemstone are Scotland and the north-east coast of England, especially Whitby bay. Though prized by ancient civilisations, including the Egyptians and Romans, it gained hugely in popularity during the Victorian period, when Queen Victoria's black mourning clothes included jewellery made from jet.

Jet is believed to have protective properties and to lend strength to those in need of it.

Pearl

Pearls are organic, formed inside the bodies of molluscs such as oysters, clams and mussels. To distinguish a real from a fake pearl, you can very gently rub it over the front of your teeth (not the edge as this can cause damage to the pearl). A real pearl should feel slightly gritty.

There are four main types of pearl:

Freshwater pearls

Freshwater pearls are the most affordable way to own pearls. They are often sold as baroque (irregular) shaped beads.

Akoya pearls

Akoya pearls, grown off the coast of Japan, are what we think of when we imagine the classic strand of round white pearls. They have a diameter of between 4 and 10mm.

Tahitian pearls

Tahitian pearls, from French Polynesia, are naturally dark pearls up to 15mm in size. It's rare to find perfectly round Tahitian pearls, but even the baroque shapes are expensive.

South Sea pearls

South Sea pearls are among the world's largest, with sizes very occasionally exceeding 20mm, and can form in various hues of cream, white and gold. South Sea pearls are some of the most valuable, sometimes costing tens of thousands of dollars per pearl.

Because they are very soft with just 2.5 to 4.5 on the Mohs scale of hardness, gently clean pearls with a damp cloth and never use chemicals as they will ruin the finish. You should store your pearls flat to prevent the silk thread stretching, but it is recommended that you have your strand re-strung every few years regardless.

Cultured pearl earrings or a strand of pearls are a traditional gift to a new bride or a college graduate. The pearl is also the birthstone for June and the gemstone for the 30th wedding anniversary. Its ancient associations with the moon and maidenhood make pearl a symbol of purity and many still use it to regulate their emotions.

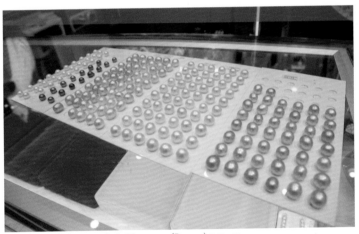

Golden South Sea pearls in Myanmar (Burma) © Kim Rix

Synthetic gemstones

We tend to have negative associations with the word 'synthetic'. We associate 'synthetic' with 'fake' or 'artificial'. So, when we hear of synthetic gems, it's tempting to dismiss them as cheap pieces of trickery.

But did you know that synthetic gems are not fakes? Synthetic gems are virtually identical to natural gems in that they have the same chemical makeup, structure, and optical and physical properties. The difference is that a natural gem forms in the earth's crust whereas a synthetic gem is formed in the lab in conditions that mimic the natural process.

Chucked together like sweets – Pick'n'Mix, Thai style © Kim Rix

Kim Rix GG (GIA)

The first benefit of synthetic gems is cost. With natural gems, the rarer the gemstone, the higher the price. A large, high quality gem can be very expensive. As synthetic gems are formed in the lab, rarity is not such an issue – but you still have a 'real' gem.

Synthetic gems are not dirt cheap, though. Remember, they are pretty much identical to natural gems. Synthetic gems vary in price depending on the process used to grow them. Some processes are more complex and costly than others.

A synthetic gem could be a good choice if you would like a gemstone with few flaws. Some gemstones, such as sapphire, ruby and emerald, have many inclusions (flaws) in their natural form. As synthetic gemstones are formed in the lab, it's easier to control the process. This means fewer inclusions.

Many people worry about whether their gemstone is an ethical purchase. There are many ways to ensure your gemstone is ethical, but if you're concerned about environmental impact or human rights issues, buying a synthetic gemstone is a very easy and straightforward way to put your mind at rest.

However, you may feel a sentimental pull towards a gemstone that has lain beneath the earth's surface for millions of years. Perhaps you *like* the fact that your gemstone has inclusions – after all, our flaws can make us unique!

Phenomenal gemstones

Phenomenal gemstones are gems with unusual optical properties, known as 'phenomena' in the world of gemmology. Chatoyancy (cat's eye), asterism (star gems), adularescence, iridescence and colour-change are phenomena caused by the way light bounces off the internal structure of a gemstone.

Adularescence
Adularescence causes the stone to appear to shimmer and glow from within and is most commonly recognised in moonstone. Found across the globe, with blue moonstone (found only in Sri Lanka) being more expensive.

Asterism (star gems)
Star gems are so called because of the six-rayed star shape that appears to float across the surface of the stone when cut as a cabochon. While the most popular star gems are sapphires and rubies, asterism can also occur in other stones, including garnet, emerald and spinel. Star gems are extremely rare and subsequently very, very costly. Beware the seller who shows you a low-priced gem exhibiting asterism — it will be a fake!

Chatoyancy (cat's eye)
Gemstones exhibiting chatoyancy appear to have a straight line floating across the surface, resembling the vertical slit pupil of a cat's eye. Be aware that an alexandrite displaying good chatoyancy will have a weak colour change — the two phenomena cannot coexist without one or both suffering.

Colour change

Colour-change gems appear to be one colour in some
lighting conditions and a different colour in others.
This is due to the way the gemstone absorbs and
reflects certain wavelengths of light from different
sources. Alexandrite, the best-known example of this
phenomena, will seem to be grass green in natural
light but rich red under artificial light. The colour change
phenomenon can also occur in sapphires and garnets.

If you're thinking of buying a colour-change gemstone, the price will
be determined by the hue and the extent of the colour change. The
most valuable colour-change gemstones will have a very distinct
colour change.

Iridescence

Iridescence is the display of rainbow colours on the
surface of the stone as the viewing angle changes.
Gemstones that display iridescence include Tahitian
pearls, opal and labradorite.

Your gemstone's setting

The metal used to set a gemstone will often reflect the value of the gemstone itself. You won't find a hugely expensive ruby set in a cheap alloy!

The metal you choose will depend on several factors.
- What looks good against this gem?
- What complements my skin tone?
- What fits with my existing wardrobe and style?
- What is suitable for the amount and type of wear this piece will need to withstand?
- What kind of setting do I want?

A good jeweller will be able to offer you constructive advice on the last two questions in particular.

The most popular metals for gemstone settings are:

Gold

Gold is a very popular metal for all types of jewellery. Gemstones are measured by carat weight, but with gold, carat refers to the purity of the metal. 24 carat gold is 99.99% pure, whereas 18 carat gold is mixed with other metal in a ratio of 18 parts to 6 parts. Gold is a very soft metal, so mixing it with harder metals makes it more suitable for regular wear. 24 carat gold is not at all suitable for jewellery! Generally, gold that is used for jewellery like rings will be about 14 carats.

The different colours of gold are produced by variations in the mixture of metals. Most popular as a colour is yellow gold, followed by white

Making gold leaf, Myanmar (Burma) © Kim Rix

gold (gold mixed with some combination of nickel) and rose gold
(gold and copper).

Palladium
Palladium is popular because it's cheaper than platinum and retains
its clean, light colour with very little maintenance. It has another
advantage for those with sensitive skin — it's hypoallergenic.

Platinum
Platinum is a popular choice both because of its sophisticated,
modern colour, but also because of its resistance to scratching. It is,
however, prone to dents if knocked hard. Rarer than gold, platinum is
correspondingly more expensive!

Sterling silver
Sterling silver is by far the most affordable precious metal and the
fact that regular wear helps silver to keep its shine makes it a
popular choice.

Gold Museum, Bogota, Colombia © Kim Rix

Kim Rix GG (GIA)

The quiet life in Corfu, Greece © Kim Rix

Kim Rix GG (GIA)

BUYING YOUR GEMSTONE

Admiring the varied colours of boulder opal, Australia © Kim Rix

Kim Rix GG (GIA)

Choosing where to buy

Now that you have thought about what you want and are armed with some information, let's have a more detailed look at where to buy!

Option 1: buying from a shop

As a tourist, the most obvious and sensible thing to do, if you are looking for a cut and polished gemstone or a piece of jewellery, is to buy from a reputable shop. This is especially true if you are intending to invest a great deal of money. Well-known shops have a reputation to protect. The gem trade in many countries is a relatively small network. News travels fast, and a bad name can mean the end of business.

Don't let your tour guide, local agent or taxi driver take you to a shop. They could well earn a commission from doing this, and you could end up paying inflated prices or, worse, being scammed.

Gems and jewellery shopping mart, Myanmar (Burma) © Kim Rix

Make sure you see the gem's **certificate** — or, if you are buying a high-end gem, its **grading report** — before you hand over any money. You'll find more about what each of these entails on pages 103 – 105 of this book. Think about the kind of establishment you are in. A shop with a reputation to uphold will have a real and serious interest in selling you genuine goods.

When weighing up whether to buy in a shop or at the market, don't forget that if there is any issue with the gemstone, you can more easily go back to a shop to complain. It is worth bearing in mind, though, that shop prices are much higher than market prices.

Depending on the country you are in, haggling may be possible in a shop. It tends not to be the case when there is a price tag on the gemstone. There is much less room for negotiation on high-end gems, as they are often significantly more expensive for the dealer or shop to acquire and cut.

Option 2: buying from a gemstone merchant
Buying your gem through a merchant will be a bit more demanding if you're a novice with no connections in the country. Gem merchants are harder to find because they don't tend to have premises at street level. Some only sell in larger quantities or to businesses. There are gemstone merchants who are happy to deal with private individuals, but you'll usually need to ring to make an appointment first. You'll often get better deals by buying directly from a gem merchant, though, so it's something worth considering.

If you already have contacts, ask them to ask around for you. It's difficult to beat personal recommendations from trusted friends and acquaintances.

Option 3: buying from an outdoor street market

If you're looking for some excitement, a challenge, and a bit of fun, buy your gemstone at one of the world's gem trading markets! The market experience in each country will be very different, so if you have a holiday destination in mind, you should also read the relevant *Gemstone Detective* book which will give you a detailed guide to buying in that particular country!

Beruwala street market, Sri Lanka © Kim Rix

Outdoor jade market, Myanmar (Burma) © Kim Rix

Rocks market, Sydney, Australia © Kim Rix

Option 4: buying at a jewellery show

This could be a great way to see a vast number of raw gems and jewellery under one roof.

Lightning Ridge Opal Show, Australia © Kim Rix

Kim Rix GG (GIA)

Option 5: buying from a gem museum

A gem museum is worth a visit if you are interested in gems and want to find out more about mining. Most also sell gemstones.

GIT Gems Museum, Bangkok, Thailand © *Kim Rix*

Prices – what to expect

Gem prices fluctuate and depend on the origin, colour, clarity, carat weight and cut of each individual gemstone. It would be difficult at best, and at worst downright misleading, to attempt to list price ranges for each stone. What you should remember is that the larger the stone, the higher the price per carat. A 5 carat ruby or sapphire would cost quite considerably more per carat than a 1 carat gem, because of its rarity.

The origin of a stone can also affect its price. Some countries have a reputation for producing gems of particularly high quality, so a gemstone from these countries will have a certain cachet. To give some examples, sapphires from Kashmir, rubies from Burma and emeralds from Colombia all tend to command a premium. This is usually because the country in question produces stones with a highly desirable colour saturation. Be aware, though, that this premium only reflects a *tendency* to quality – all mines in all countries produce gems of varying worth. You cannot rely on origin alone as an indicator of value.

A gemstone's colour – its hue, saturation and tone – is the most important indicator of value, with saturation being the more important of the three. Saturation refers to the intensity of the stone's hue: the richer the saturation, the higher the price.

You might think that stones with inclusions fetch a lower price than stones with excellent clarity. This is generally true. However, some stones are deemed *more* valuable when they have particular inclusions. Amber which contains a fossilized insect is highly prized, and horsetail inclusions in Russian demantoid garnet are very much sought after.

Cut tends not to influence price as much as colour and clarity. However, it does still have a significant effect on the value of a gem.

Because rarer gemstones are often cut to preserve as much weight as possible, the proportions of the cut can sometimes fall short. It may be worth having a wonky ruby, sapphire or emerald recut if enhancing the stone's beauty will add more value than is lost through having less carat weight. Cheaper gemstones tend to be cut extremely well as carat weight is not such an issue.

Cuts like marquise result in more wastage, which is why such cuts are less common in valuable gemstones. The Asscher cut is the most expensive of all — not because the cut itself is worth more, but because it only looks good on very high quality stones with minimal flaws. See page 117 for more details on popular cuts.

One more thing to consider is the '**brand**' of a stone. A gemstone or jewellery brand's good reputation and ubiquity mean customers are prepared to pay more for the reassurance of buying from a well-known supplier.

Ametrine ZigZag, cut by John Dyer. Photography © Ozzie Campos

Negotiating – when and how to do it

Negotiating a price for your gemstone is generally acceptable at a gem market and may be tolerated in a shop, depending on the country and the kind of establishment it is.

How to strike a deal at a gem market
If you're intending to buy at the market, you'll need to know a bit about how it all works. Navigating the market can be daunting for a beginner and it almost certainly won't look like the marketplace of a sleepy English town!

The gem markets of each country tend to differ slightly in the way they work. You might find trading offices with buyers and dealers sitting at tables, or individual dealers standing around selling off the back of mopeds. Wherever you are, you'll see a lot of dealers selling to each other, and many people wearing head torches and head goggles (magnifying glasses). It may well be hot, and it'll almost certainly be noisy and crowded.

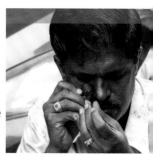

Using a loupe © Kim Rix

Gem market, Myanmar (Burma) © Kim Rix

Kim Rix GG (GIA)

Gem market, Chantaburi, Thailand © Kim Rix

So how do you go about it?

1. Lose the tourist look:

If you were visiting London's Hatton Garden or
New York's 47th Street, I would give you the same,
commonsense, advice! Don't let the dazzling
array of gemstones on display distract you from
personal security. Keep your camera, handbag,
wallet and phone close by and hidden or don't take
them at all.

2. Remember the rules:

Keep a **level head** when shown the seller's stones. Look at them one
by one and if you don't want any of them, be **firm but polite**. Say "No
thanks", and give a **reason** for your decision, for example, "It's not big
enough" or "It's not the right colour." Let the seller collect their stones to
avoid any confusion or — in the worst case — accusations of theft. Be

aware of and control where you see the stones – e.g. not above a drain.

Whatever country you're in, the key is to remain **polite, firm and in control**. Don't be rude, don't get hot and bothered, and don't let yourself get pushed and shoved around.

3. Negotiate price:
At most gem markets, you can reduce asking prices — sometimes by a significant amount — but you'll need good negotiating skills! Here are some general bargaining tips:

- Let the seller name a price first
- Start with a much lower counter offer
- Say as little as possible — make the seller do the work
- Privately set yourself a price limit and don't go beyond it. Be prepared to walk away

English is spoken in many countries, but be prepared for sellers who do not know it. Be prepared to negotiate wordlessly. In some countries this is done by writing figures on a piece of paper or calculator and passing it between them.

Cutting and polishing gemstones © Kim Rix

Kim Rix GG (GIA)

4. Get it tested and certified:

The most difficult aspect of buying at a gemstone market is identifying whether a gemstone is natural, synthetic or imitation. With all the excitement, heat and pressure it's easy to give in to buying before you check. DON'T! **Make sure it is real**. You must make sure you are not being sold a less valuable stone or, worse, something out of a Christmas cracker!

Don't be fooled by alternative names. Bohemian rubies are NOT real rubies but semi-precious garnets. Water sapphire is NOT sapphire, but iolite. If the gemstone is preceded by an unexpected description, be prepared to walk away! You can find a list of misleading gem names on page 96.

If there is a gem lab within walking distance, a market seller should be happy to walk with you to it so that you can get confirmation of the gem's identity. In the world's most established gem markets, you might find a mobile lab. It may be possible to get a simple verbal confirmation that the stone is what the seller says it is, rather than have to wait for a detailed report.

Agate display, Australia © Kim Rix

Polishing jade, Myanmar (Burma) © *Kim Rix*

Kim Rix GG (GIA)

Gemstones as investments

Is it a good idea to buy a gemstone as an investment? If you ask the opinion of three different people, you'll probably get three different answers.

There is no simple answer to this question and you should bear in mind that all investments involve some degree of risk. That said, a diversified portfolio carries less risk than putting all of your eggs in one basket, so why not include a precious stone or two alongside your other assets?

Gemstones are hard assets, like a property or cash. Historically, they have acted as a hedge against inflation and as a safe haven during financial crises (when stocks and bonds fall).

Gemstones do increase in value, but it's a long-term game. Gemstone prices fluctuate, like any investment. Over the long term, however, gemstones have risen in value significantly. Nevertheless, be aware that they will not be as easy to liquidate as other assets, should you need cash in a hurry!

With all this in mind, if you wish to buy a gemstone as an investment, buy only the best quality.

My advice would be to buy a gemstone that you like and will be pleased to wear, rather than something to be locked away in a safe and hardly ever seen. Buy a gemstone that speaks to you.

Unfortunately, there are too many people only happy to help you part with your hard-earned cash. If you are serious about investing, I strongly recommend that you seek the advice of a financial advisor before you part with large amounts of money.

The ethics of buying gemstones

These days, tourists are thankfully more aware of the ethical issues that dog the gemstone industry. Human rights abuses and the environmental impact of large-scale mining are things that should be foremost in our minds when buying gemstones at home and abroad. We need to know that our business is supporting rather than exploiting people.

On my travels, I have met and come to know many people who depend on artisanal mining to support their families. It's these small businesses that really suffer when confidence in the gem trade is low. If we stop buying from the small-scale mines, livelihoods are destroyed. When abroad, I have made it my mission to build long-term relationships with people I trust — people who are doing the right thing by their workers and their environment.

Conflict diamonds
Even if you are not a diamond connoisseur, you will probably have heard the term 'conflict' or 'blood' diamonds and be aware that diamonds have been fuelling civil wars. Sierra Leone, Liberia, Angola, the Republic of Congo, Côte d'Ivoire, the Central African Republic, and the Democratic Republic of Congo have all been embroiled in violent civil discord over recent years, driven by diamonds.

A conflict diamond is defined as an illegally traded diamond mined at some point within the last 50 years.

Established by the United Nations in the year 2003, the Kimberly Process was designed to prevent conflict diamonds from entering the mainstream diamond market. It enables legitimate traders to certify their diamonds as 'conflict free'. Even so, these illegal diamonds still slip through the net, with some estimating that up to 15% of diamonds sold in mainstream markets are conflict diamonds. It's also important to note that the Kimberly Process doesn't exclude diamonds mined in a way that damages communities, the environment or the miners themselves.

How to buy an ethical diamond

1. Find out the source. Ask your jeweller where the diamonds were mined.

2. Ask for details about the diamonds.

3. Don't buy diamonds that come from countries notorious for human rights abuses in their mining industry. Check Amnesty International and Human Rights Watch if you're not sure.

4. You might end up paying a bit more, but buy diamonds in countries where standards are rigorously enforced – Canada, for example.

5. Support the miners in Namibia and Botswana, and other countries where miners' rights and environmental standards are strictly enforced. Income from mining creates jobs and will help these developing countries.

6. Buy from a reputable dealer who will guarantee that each diamond was mined with stringent criteria on responsible and ethical sourcing.

7. Buy from jewellers who make a commitment to ethical sourcing.

Pearl Farming

Did you know that it takes about 10,000 pearls to find enough matching stones for a pearl necklace? That's a lot of oysters, and many believe that this amounts to cruel exploitation of animals.

Pearls are formed when the oyster or other mollusc secretes a substance called nacre around an irritant that has found its way into the mollusc's shell. Over time, layers of nacre build up to become a pearl. With cultured pearls, the farmer inserts the irritant into the mollusc's gonads rather than waiting for it to happen naturally.

Some avoid pearls for environmental reasons, as large-scale oyster farming has contributed to the destruction of natural oyster beds.

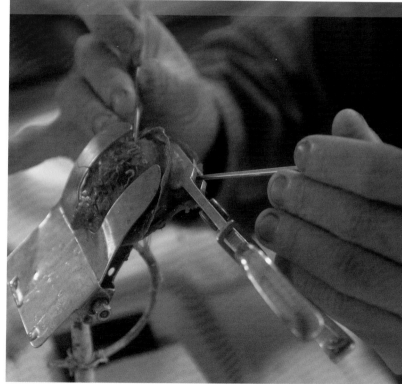

Spare a thought for the poor oyster © *Lauriane Pinsault*

Coral jewellery

Precious coral takes a long time to form and is therefore very difficult to farm sustainably. There is ongoing argument in countries such as Spain over measures taken to protect coral stocks. As we become more aware of the damage that humans are doing to the ocean, increasing numbers of jewellers have decided not to use coral in their designs.

Kim Rix GG (GIA)

Top 10 questions to ask before you buy

1. **What is this stone called?**
   Check your list of fake names!

2. **Is it natural, or synthetic?**
   If natural, has it been treated in any way?

3. **Where is this stone from?**
   A gem's country of origin can affect its value potential.

4. **Does it come with a lab report or shop certificate of authenticity?**
   If not, will the seller allow you to have it tested before you buy?

5. **What's its hardness?**
   Some gems are easily scratched and so not suitable for everyday pieces of jewellery, especially rings and bracelets.

6. **Are you registered with a gem trade association (trade governing body)?**

7. **What's your returns/refund policy?**

8. **How do I care for my gem?**

9. **As a tourist, can I claim back the tax on my gemstone? If so, will you give me a receipt to claim tax back at the airport?**
   Not all businesses are registered for VAT/sales tax.

10. **How long will my jewellery take to make?**
    Make sure the jeweller knows your deadline!

Buying gemstones and jewellery around the world

- Not all shop assistants are gemmologists, or even interested in what they are selling.

- Watch where you're standing. Always view gemstones with a soft ground below.

- Good gemstones like diamonds, emeralds, ruby and sapphire are usually sold with a GIA certificate.

- Keep asking questions. Don't wait for information to be offered to you.

- Be aware that your guide or local agent may well get a commission if they take you directly to a shop or dealer and you buy from there.

- If you suspect the price has been artificially inflated to allow for tourists wanting to haggle, make to leave and you will soon find out.

Kim Rix GG (GIA)

- Remember that many labs will not test rough stones or polished gemstones already set in jewellery.

- Use the torch on your mobile phone to check the clarity of gemstones.

- Many gemstones will appear different in different lights. Always look at gemstones in neutral light — that's midday light on a bright day.

- Flawless gemstones are very rare. A flawless stone at a low price should arouse suspicion.

- Country of origin isn't always the best place to buy. For example, if you're looking for a good deal on a diamond, be aware that diamonds are cheaper in larger, more competitive markets like Mumbai and New York.

Checking clarity with a mobile phone © Kim Rix

Junkanoo Carnival, Nassau, Bahamas © *Kim Rix*

Kim Rix GG (GIA)

8ct natural Burmese ruby for £300 – too good to be true? © Kim Rix

Kim Rix GG (GIA)

IDENTIFYING SCAMS AND FAKES

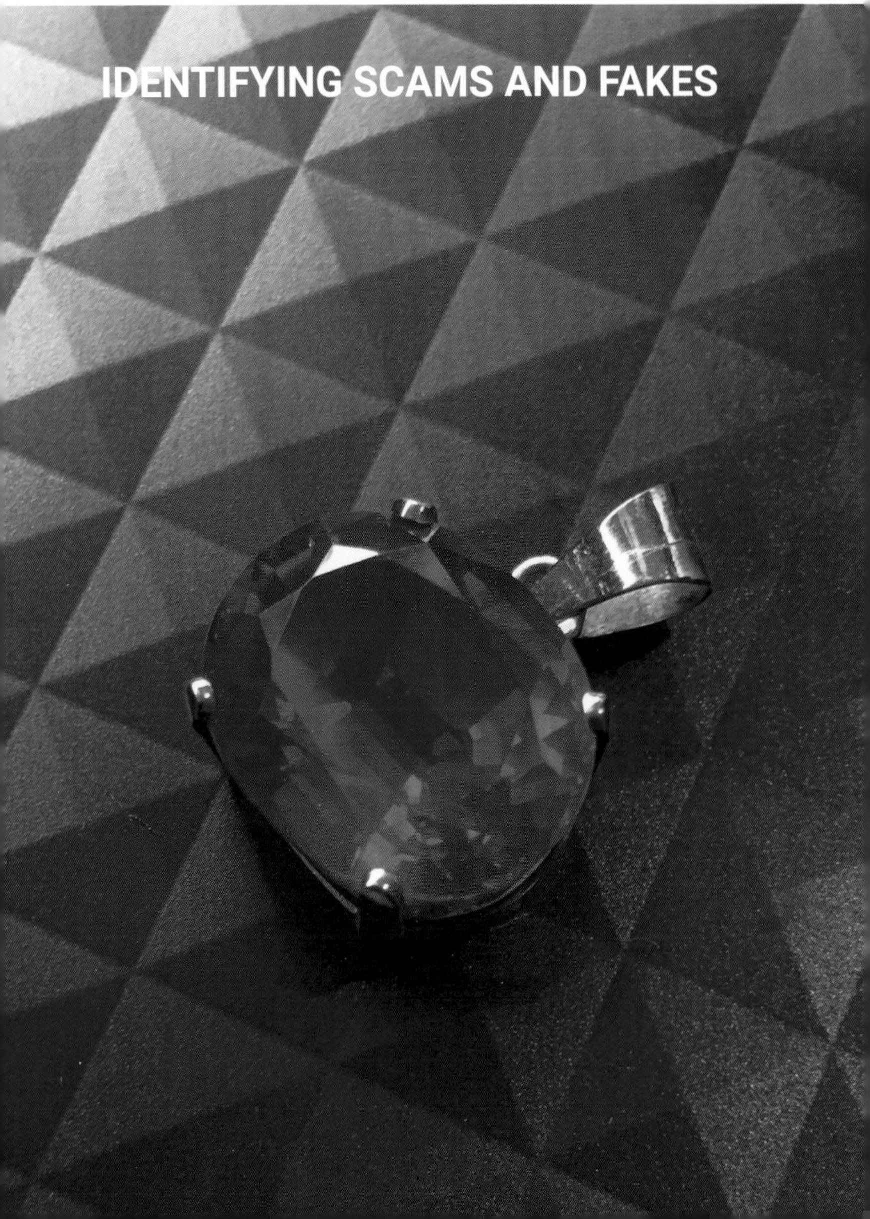

Cutting ruby in Thailand © Kim Rix

Kim Rix GG (GIA)

Categories of gemstones

There are six categories of gemstone you need to be aware of:

1. Natural, untreated gemstones

Top of the range are natural, untreated gemstones. 'Natural' means they were formed in the earth, and 'untreated' means they have not had anything done to enhance their beauty besides being cut and set. Because of their rarity, these can cost thousands of pounds and you should expect them to come with a lab report.

2. Natural gemstone and treated

Next in line are heat-treated stones. In the grand scheme of things, 95% of *all* gemstones sold have been treated in some way but the figure is closer to 99% for stones such as rubies and sapphires. Heat treatment is the norm for some stones, aiming to enhance their colour and clarity.

Heating is the most common gemstone treatment, but other treatments may be used to enhance the appearance of a gemstone. These include bleaching (e.g. pearls and jadeite jade), dying (e.g. pearls, emerald, ruby) and oiling (e.g. emeralds).

3. Fracture or fissure treatment

However, you do need to be aware of fracture/fissure-treated stones (also known as glass-filled stones) where, in addition to heat treatment, cracks within the stone have had a glass-like substance injected into them. This method can significantly improve the appearance of a low-quality sapphire that would not otherwise be considered gem quality. However, it introduces the risk that, when exposed to heat in the jewellery mounting process, the filling can melt out of the stone and ruin its appearance.

Synthetic gemstones, Bangkok, Thailand © Kim Rix

4. Synthetic or created gemstones

The term 'synthetic' properly refers to a stone with the same physical and chemical properties as a natural stone, but which was created in a lab rather than in the earth.

Confusingly, some people use the term 'synthetic' interchangeably with 'simulated', which means 'fake'. Always make sure you know what you're buying! True synthetic (created) stones are not *always* cheaper than a natural stone — it depends on the quality of the stone in question.

Many people prefer synthetic stones because they have fewer inclusions, and their carbon footprint is smaller than stones mined using industrial machinery. Others believe that synthetic stones lack the interest, history and romance of a gemstone formed underground over billions of years. The best decision is the one that feels right for you!

Kim Rix GG (GIA)

5. Composite or assembled gems

A composite or assembled gemstone is a single stone made from different materials. The term can refer to slightly different treatments. Some composite gems are composed of a thin slice of gemstone attached to another, less valuable, substance to enhance the gem's appearance and stability. Such stones are often called **doublets** or **triplets**, depending on the number of layers used. The layer of gemstone will be thinner in a triplet than in a doublet.

Composite can also refer to a type of treatment performed on corundum, the mineral otherwise known as ruby or sapphire. Composite rubies and sapphires are formed in the lab, using an acid treatment to remove the inclusions in a piece of low-quality corundum that would otherwise be of little use. The substantial holes left behind are then filled in with as much lead glass as is required. Lead glass is softer than normal glass and composite stones often contain more than 40% of this material, which makes the stone very vulnerable. If you decide to get the gem professionally cleaned, re-set or its ring re-sized, or even if you wear your jewellery while cleaning or cooking, a composite ruby could easily be damaged irreparably.

Buying a composite gem *is* fine if you know what you're buying *and* have paid an appropriately low price for it. The problems come when dealers knowingly – or unknowingly – try to sell you a composite as a real gemstone. A trained eye with good lighting and a jeweller's loupe *might* be able to identify a composite, but the only way to be absolutely sure is to have the stone tested in an independent lab.

Synthetic opal © Kim Rix

6. Imitation or simulation gemstone

Imitations or simulations are fakes. The terms refer to a cheaper material made to look like a more expensive gem. Fake doesn't always mean the stone is glass, however — it might be a less valuable gemstone sold as a more expensive one. For example, garnet is sometimes sold as ruby and iolite as sapphire.

Pyramids at Giza, near Cairo, Egypt © Kim Rix

Kim Rix GG (GIA)

Common scams

Scams have been around on this earth for as long as goods have been sold. As a tourist, you're more vulnerable to these tricks. It's the most natural thing in the world to trust a friendly-looking face, but you should always remain cautious if your safety or your money are at stake!

An extra word of caution here: DON'T fall into the trap of trusting complete strangers because they look like expats or fellow tourists helping you out. Fraudsters are fraudsters, even if they speak with the same language and accents as you. (One of your compatriots could be in on the act!)

There are as many tricks as there are confidence tricksters, but if you are aware of how some of the world's most common gemstone scams work, you'll have a far greater chance of identifying a dodgy sale.

 ### The Straightforward Scam

Far and away the most common way to get scammed is simply by buying a stone that isn't what you think it is. Whether it's a piece of coloured glass, a treated gemstone masquerading as a natural one, a low value mineral being sold as a different gemstone altogether, unless you have your gemstone tested in an independent lab, there's no completely foolproof way of sorting the real from the replica. The information in this book is designed to help you get a feel for when something's not quite right. Ultimately, though, you'll need to rely on your gut instinct or an independent lab.

Pure silver from Myanmar (Burma) © Kim Rix

Kim Rix GG (GIA)

The Sneaky Switch

Another popular trick around the world is to go through a big show of having you examine a gemstone under a light and magnification, brandishing its lab report and then surreptitiously switching the stone for something less valuable at the point of sale. Keep a close eye on what's happening and don't let yourself get distracted by what's going on around you.

 ### The Devious Display

Think about how the stones are displayed. Make sure you have an opportunity to examine the gemstone under neutral lighting conditions – in lay-person's terms, that's the kind of light you get on a bright day at noon. The type of light affects our perception of colour, so careful lighting is one way that sellers can enhance the perceived value of a gem. Rubies can be made to look a deeper red, sapphires a more intense blue, and so on.

 ### The Captive Audience

Getting a customer through the shop door is often the biggest hurdle a dealer has to overcome. It's very easy to be swayed by a persuasive salesperson and so if you notice that you're a captive audience, be extra vigilant. Even if the stone isn't a fake, it's likely to be significantly overpriced. Cruise ships, holiday resort gift shops and guided tours that end with a visit to a shop are all good ways of getting a tourist to part with more cash than they might otherwise have done.

The Special Offer

A classic sales technique is to place a time limited deal on a product. This is all totally legitimate, of course, but scammers use this type of sales psychology too. One well-worn trick is to tell the gullible tourist that today is the last day of a sales period. The tourist, pressured into a hasty purchase, is less likely to approach the sale with caution.

 ### The Government Scheme

In this scam, a friendly taxi driver politely asks whether you'd mind pretending to look around a gem shop. He tells you that there's a government scheme to boost profit from tourism — if he takes you to a gem shop, he can get money off his fuel/taxes/food etc. Once you're there, it's hard to resist the sales pressure. Even if you do end up buying a genuine gemstone, the taxi driver will have made a commission on your purchase and you are likely to have paid more than your souvenir is worth.

Kim Rix GG (GIA)

The Closed Attraction

Variations of this trick are popular in cities with famous tourist attractions. Seeing you heading in the direction of the museum/temple/palace, a friendly chap — maybe a local or a fellow tourist — lets you know that today the attraction is closed. After engaging you in conversation, he looks at his watch and says he has time to show you a couple of local sites of interest. Grateful for his time and help, you let your guard down and so when, after a while, he tells you about the incredible wholesale deals to be had at a nearby gem exporters' trade fair, you decide you may as well take a look. Once there, it's easy to be beguiled by the prospect of snapping up a bargain. Of course, once you get home and have your purchases valued, they turn out to be worth a fraction of what you paid for them.

The False Friend

Our natural human tendency to warm to a friendly face means it's easy to put too much trust in someone you've just met. A false friend may indeed be someone downright dishonest, but a person's motivation and intentions are often much more complicated than that. Remember that in many countries, poverty is a big problem. Tourists are often seen as fair game because they are wealthy by comparison. It is certainly possible to strike up what feels like a genuinely friendly relationship — an invitation to dinner, an introduction to the family — and still end up out of pocket, whether this is maliciously done or not.

The duty-free Deception

As with all scams there are many variations of the duty-free scam, all of them based on a using a tourist's duty-free allowance. You may get talking to someone who says they (or their friend/family member) own a jewellery business. They ask if you can ship the gems to an address on their behalf, using your duty-free allowance to help them save money on export duty. You won't have to pay anything, they assure you, and they will give you a generous payment for helping them out.

Here's where it gets messy. You are warned that you might get a call from the customs department and sure enough, a day or two after posting the package, that call arrives. The 'customs officer' accuses you of fraud and threatens to have you arrested if you can't show proof of purchase. In a panic you call your new friend, who says it's safest to make a payment. They will reimburse you once their contact receives the package.

The business contact and customs officer are, of course, a complete fabrication and you are very unlikely to see that money again.

Tourists have been scammed out of vast sums of money in this way, even those who are usually sensible and cautious. Greed and fear make a dangerous combination — don't let the desire to make a quick buck get in the way of your common sense!

Kim Rix GG (GIA)

Fake gems

Is your gemstone real?

The chapter **'Knowing what you're looking at'** gives you the essentials, but you must be aware that even an expert can't tell for sure with the naked eye whether a stone is genuine. Some imitations are very convincing. Arm yourself with a jeweller's **loupe** (a small magnifying glass) and list of clues, however, and you could save yourself some time and expense by rejecting the more obviously fake rubies and sapphires. Jeweller's loupes are readily available online, and in countries famous for their gem trade you can buy them in plenty of shops. 10x magnification with a triplet lens is the type recommended by gemmologists and the type that you will find for sale on www.gemstonedetective.com.

These tests are NOT definitive. They may help uncover a fake, but they should **never** be used on their own as 'proof' that your gemstone is real! The only way to be sure is to have your gemstone tested by an independent lab.

Clue 1: look for inclusions

If you are able to examine your gem through a jeweller's loupe, you will probably see small inclusions (flaws) in a genuine stone. It's next to impossible to replicate the flaws of a natural stone in synthetic or imitation stones. Naturally flawless stones are extremely rare and correspondingly eye-wateringly expensive!

Australian sapphires © *Rubyvale Gem Gallery*

Don't confuse natural inclusions with the gas bubbles often visible in a composite gemstone. Bubbles indicate that the 'gemstone' has been formed artificially by combining low quality material with lead glass.

Clue 2: consider the price
Is the price too good to be true? If you are shown a 'genuine' gemstone at what seems like an attractively low price, it is likely to be a fake. Fake doesn't necessarily have to mean glass — it could mean that a less valuable, semi-precious stone has been substituted for the real thing. Garnet and tourmaline are often used in place of ruby, and iolite as a substitute for sapphire. However lovely they are as gemstones in their own right, they are not what you are paying for!

Clue 3: look at the colour
This is harder for the amateur to discern. A genuine gemstone will have a brilliance, a glow, to it that fakes tend not to have. Glass gemstones don't dazzle in the same way.

Clue 4: examine the surface

Very hard gemstones such as diamond, ruby and sapphire are extremely resistant to scratching. If you see any scratching or abrasion on the surface, alarm bells should ring. The edges of these stones should be crisp and sharp, not rounded or damaged. Beware, though! A surface with sharp edges and no scratches does not necessarily mean your stone is what the seller says it is.

Clue 5: and...breathe!

If you breathe gently on a real diamond, ruby or sapphire, the condensation should take only a second to disappear. On a glass fake, it tends to take longer — five or so seconds.

Precious gemstones for sale, Ratnapura, Sri Lanka © Kim Rix

Misleading names and their true meaning

 Don't let a misleading name beguile you into buying a stone worth less than you think it is!

Fake alexandrite:

Blue alexandrite   colour-change sapphire

Fake amethyst:

Japanese amethyst   synthetic amethyst

Fake aquamarine:

Brazilian aquamarine   blue-green topaz

Fake diamond:

Alaskan black diamond	hematite
Herkimer diamond	colourless quartz
Matura diamond	colourless zircon
Mogok diamond	colourless topaz
Rangoon diamond	colourless zircon

Fake emerald:

Chatham emerald	synthetic
Gilson emerald	synthetic
Oriental emerald	green sapphire

Fake jade:

Australian jade	chrysoprase quartz
Indian jade	aventurine quartz
Korean jade	serpentine
Manchurian jade	soapstone
Mexican jade	dyed green calcite
Soochow jade	serpentine, soapstone

Fake lapis lazuli:

German lapis	dyed-blue jasper
Swiss lapis	dyed-blue jasper

Fake pearl:

Atlas pearl	imitation
Red sea pearl	coral

Fake ruby:

Adelaide ruby	garnet
Australian ruby	garnet
Balas ruby	spinel
Bohemian ruby	garnet
Brazilian ruby	tourmaline
Cape ruby	garnet

Fake sapphire:

Lux sapphire	iolite
Water sapphire	iolite

Fake topaz:

Madeira topaz	quartz
Palmeira topaz	quartz
Rio topaz	quartz
Smoky topaz	smoky quartz

FairGems working mine, Sri Lanka © Kim Rix

Kim Rix GG (GIA)

Cocktail hour! Punta Cana, Dominican Republic © *Kim Rix*

Kim Rix GG (GIA)

A beautiful cushion cut spinel © Kim Rix

Kim Rix GG (GIA)

Certificates of authenticity and grading reports

A gemstone's value depends on many factors, which vary from gemstone to gemstone. However, a good rule of thumb is this: the rarer, the bigger and the more naturally beautiful a gemstone is, the more it will be worth. The problem is that you cannot fully analyse a stone with just the naked eye or gemmologist's **loupe** (magnifying glass).

This is where the gem labs come in. In a gem lab, experts using high-tech equipment will be able to give you a lot of information about your stone.

The cost of having your stone analysed in a lab will vary. Some (not all) may offer identification of your gemstone with a simple verbal confirmation. This is a good budget option if you just want to know whether your stone is genuine or not. A grading report, with more detailed information about the stone, will be more expensive.

Something you need to be clear about is the difference between a **certificate of authenticity** and a **grading report**.

Certificate of authenticity

A certificate of authenticity is a written guarantee that your gemstone is what the seller says it is. It does not contain much specific detail about the stone. A certificate is there to reassure you that you're getting a genuine gemstone and not a chunk of glass. Many gems, especially those bought in shops, hotels or museums, will be sold with such a certificate.

Whether this certificate is trustworthy is another matter. It's very easy to create an official-looking certificate of authenticity simply by downloading a template from the internet. Ultimately, you will have to use your own judgement about the respectability of the establishment.

AGTL Gemstone report, Beruwala, Sri Lanka © Kim Rix

Grading report

A grading report (which, confusingly, is sometimes referred to as a certificate!) gives a **detailed analysis** of a gemstone and is carried out in a gemmological laboratory. It will provide you with a written assessment of your gemstone according to several criteria: carat weight, saturation, hue, tone, brilliance, clarity, and the type of treatment it has undergone. You probably won't want to bother having this done unless you are spending a lot of money. Expensive gemstones from high-end shops will tend to come with a grading report anyway. If you do want to get the more detailed grading report for your gem, this can take up to 7 days, which may not suit your holiday schedule.

A grading report can also tell you your stone's country of origin. This can have a bearing on the value of the gemstone because some countries have become associated with the quality of particular stones. For example, a Burmese ruby will fetch more than an otherwise equivalent ruby from Tanzania.

Note that gem labs cannot perform certain tests on rough stones or stones that have already been set in jewellery. If the gemstone has already been set into a piece of jewellery, it may well need to be removed by a jeweller and then re-set after the test. Ask your gem lab about submission requirements.

In some labs the cost of a grading report or certificate of authenticity will depend on the carat weight of the gem. Others have a more standardised price list.

Some labs give you the option of an express service and will be able to produce a grading report within hours.

Before you take your gemstone for testing, be aware of the following:

- Laboratories certify gemstones, but **no one certifies laboratories**. Gem labs stand on their reputation alone.

- There is **no standard method for testing gemstones**. Each lab will have its own process and so it is possible that the same gemstone, tested at different labs, could come back with slightly different reports.

- **Beware of labs issuing grading reports which are in fact certificates/appraisals**. A full grading report will include an assessment of the origin, colour, clarity, treatments and the final quality grading of your gemstone. Note that testing the origin of your gemstone may mean paying an additional fee.

- Always **check that the lab name on your report is the same all the way through the document**. The cover on your report might come from a well-known and established lab, but the pages inside from a lab with a very slightly altered name. Sometimes the difference is very subtle.

World's most widely-recognised gem labs

The following gem labs are internationally renowned for their gemstone analysis and gemmological research.

Gemological Institute of America (GIA)
World Headquarters
Address: The Robert Mouawad Campus, 5345 Armada Drive, Carlsbad, California 92008, USA
Tel: +1 (800) 421 7250 or (760) 603 4000
Web: www.gia.edu

International Gemological Institute (IGI)
Address: 579 Fifth Avenue, New York, NY 10017, USA
Tel: +1 (212) 753 7100
Web: www.igiworldwide.com

Gubelin Gemological Laboratories
Locations in Lucerne, Hong Kong and New York
Web: www.gubelin.com/en/gemmology/gemlab

American Gemological Laboratories (AGL)
Address: 580 5th Ave Suite 706, New York, NY 10036, USA
Tel: +1 (212) 704 0727
Web: www.aglgemlab.com

Cenote near Chichen Itza, Mexico © Kim Rix

Kim Rix GG (GIA)

Lively and fun Greek nights © *Kim Rix*

Kim Rix GG (GIA)

Caribbean wedding vibes © Kim Rix

Kim Rix GG (GIA)

Getting a piercing on holiday

You've left the office far behind you and you're feeling super relaxed. Seized by the urge to celebrate your holiday and inspired by the gorgeous body jewellery you've seen, you decide to get a piercing. Ears, nose, lips, eyebrow, belly button, tongue... or even somewhere more daring!

However carefree and bohemian the barman's eyebrow ring looks, body piercing is a serious business. There is a lot to consider and you should think carefully about the decision. Ask yourself the following:

Where on my body should I have my piercing?
Don't forget to take your lifestyle and personal pain threshold into account. If your work uniform has a close-fitting waistband, a belly piercing might not be such a good idea. Earlobes are the least painful place to have pierced as they have fewer nerve endings. Nipples, on the other hand, are particularly sensitive!

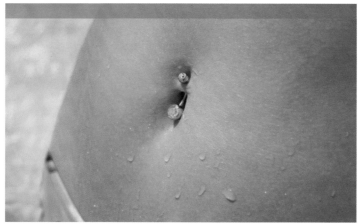

Belly piercing

Who should I trust to do my body piercing?
It goes without saying that you should never entrust your piercing to just anyone. Don't be seduced by a low price or a pretty piece of jewellery. We all know the dangers of unhygienic equipment and shared needles. Make sure you go to a licensed body piercing shop or piercer. Even if they do have the paperwork, trust your instincts and walk away if you're not happy. Your health is at risk!

 In the UK and some other countries, it is illegal to use a piercing gun other than on the ear lobes. A reputable piercer won't use a gun, even for ear lobes, as the gun cannot be sterilized.

What style of body piercing is best for my body?
Curved or straight bar, long or short — it all depends on your body. Make sure you get the right type and size body jewellery, or your piercing will be uncomfortable and difficult to care for.

Remember your piercing is essentially an open wound, so you will need to be careful about the type of metal used. Make sure your new body jewellery is not made of silver, zinc, nickel or any other low-grade metal to avoid oxidisation, irritation or rejection of the piercing. The best metals to use are surgical grade titanium and surgical steel.

How will I need to care for my piercing?
Feeling chilled out doesn't mean you can relax about looking after your piercing. Think about the activities you're planning to do — are they compatible with a freshly pierced body part that's more vulnerable to infection?

Proposing on holiday

Will you marry me? © *Charles Dardenne, Clovis Pictures*

Congratulations! There are few things in life as romantic and memorable as going down on one knee while on holiday, and if you're planning to pop the question, why not do it with a ring from the country you're in? It's a beautiful way to keep the memories of your holiday with you forever.

Of course, diamonds are traditional, forever and a girl's best friend. But there are plenty of other choices out there. In fact, Walter Schumann's *Gemstones of the World* lists about 200 different varieties of natural gemstones. You could choose a stone particularly associated with your holiday destination: for example, golden sapphire is unique to Thailand, tanzanite to Tanzania and parti sapphire to Australia. Or you might want a ring that symbolises your favourite holiday memory: a ruby to remind you of spectacular sunsets; an aquamarine to represent the sea and surf; or a peridot to reflect hikes in green hills and lush forests.

Do think about the durability of the gemstone. An engagement ring is worn every day and being on the hand means it's prone to a few knocks and scratches. Don't forget to ask the vendor about the gemstone's hardness, toughness and stability (see page 135).

Make sure you've read the sections in this book that cover the buying process before you hand over any money and familiarise yourself with the warning signs of a bad deal.

Apart from this, there are no hard and fast rules. Go for the gemstone that speaks to you both and remember that its size, style, price and setting is no one else's business but yours.

Ring styles

If you're overwhelmed by all the choice, you could start by considering the two most popular styles of engagement ring:

Tiffany-style ring

This style is about the setting, not the stone, and was popularised by the famous New York jewellery store. In a Tiffany-style ring, a single stone (often a diamond) is raised up and held securely on top of the band by four or six prongs.

Trilogy ring

Trilogy rings have three stones and are also known as past, present, future rings because that's exactly what they symbolise — a couple's past, present and future.

If you want to have something created using your own vision and personal preferences, visit your chosen jeweller at the beginning of your holiday. Don't wait until the end and have the last-minute stress of getting it perfect.

Popular engagement ring cuts
The cut of the stone is also something you'll want to consider. If you can't decide which cut you'd like based on looks alone, why not pick one that embodies your beloved's personality?

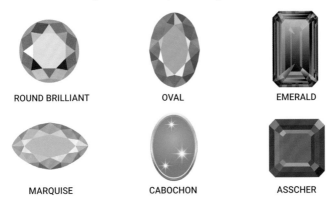

ROUND BRILLIANT   OVAL   EMERALD

MARQUISE   CABOCHON   ASSCHER

Round Brilliant cut
The round brilliant cut is a bestseller, as it combines a classic shape with a cutting style designed to produce maximum sparkle. People who choose this cut tend to be happy, sociable and content in their own skin. They don't feel that they need to mark themselves out as being 'different' as they're fine with who they are.

Oval cut
The oval cut has become even more popular after Prince William presented Kate Middleton with his mother's oval cut sapphire ring. Those who love an oval cut ring are probably refined and classy with a great sense of classic style.

Emerald cut

Not just for emeralds any more, this cut is great to show off a gem's depth of colour. The stepped cut became popular in the art deco period. If you find yourself drawn to this cut, you're a deep thinker — possibly even an introvert — and love chic, stylish accessories.

Marquise cut

The marquise cut is an oval with pointed ends — sometimes described as a boat or eye shape. It's a vintage cut and less common in engagement rings than it used to be. If the boat-shaped gem floats your boat, you'll probably lean towards an unusual, eclectic style. You're sharp-witted and don't suffer fools gladly.

Cabochon cut

The cabochon cut is a rounded shape with no facets. It's often seen on stones like moonstone and opal or any gem with striking patterns or variations. A cabochon cut is great for a romantic and a dreamer who likes floaty, feminine styles and may even be a bit of a hippy at heart!

Asscher cut

The Asscher cut is a square, stepped cut popular in diamond engagement rings because its high crown and large, stepped facets produce a brilliant 'hall of mirrors' effect. It's expensive because this cut won't disguise flaws in the same way as a round cut can. The Asscher cut is definitely one for a high-flyer or perfectionist.

Choosing a diamond engagement ring

I've lost count of the number of men who tell me they wish they'd known more about diamonds before proposing. You don't need to be an expert to buy a diamond engagement ring, but it helps to go into it armed with a bit of information. First, let's look at how the Four Cs – colour, clarity, cut and carat weight – relate to diamonds.

Colour

Colour is graded according to a scale from D (colourless) to Z (light yellow). The yellower the diamond, the lower the price. Remember that the colour of the setting can affect how you perceive the diamond's colour! Use platinum or white gold for colour grades D-J, and yellow gold for lower colour grades.

GIA COLOR SCALE

Diamond colour scale © *Courtesy of the Gemological Institute of America (GIA)*

Clarity

Clarity is measured against an 11-point scale ranging from Flawless (F) to Included (I). At the lower end of this scale, inclusions will be obvious under 10x magnification and may affect the diamond's brilliance and transparency.

Cut

Cut is the most important factor affecting the appearance of a diamond, so it's worth going for the best quality you can afford. The quality of cut is categorised from Excellent to Poor and should be

---

listed on the diamond's certificate. A well-executed round brilliant cut is the type to choose if you're looking for maximum sparkle.

Carat weight
The higher the carat weight, the higher the price per carat. Popular sizes attract a premium, so choose a diamond that's just under a carat boundary. A diamond of 0.95 carats looks very similar to a 1.00 carat diamond but could cost you 20-30% less.

Top tips to make your money go further

- To get to a price point you can afford, first reduce clarity, then colour grade and finally the cut quality

- Use lower carat gold for the setting

- Pair a lower colour grade with yellow gold to make the diamond seem whiter by comparison

- Choose a stone just below one of the carat boundaries, e.g. at 0.50, 0.70, 0.90, 1.00 and 1.50 carats

- Instead of a larger single diamond (a solitaire), spread the carat weight across three or more smaller stones

World famous jewellery collections

Beautiful collections or displays of gemstones and jewellery can be found all over the world and to name them all would make this book far too big for your pocket or handbag! However, if you're interested in seeing some truly spectacular exhibitions, here are some of the world's most famous collections:

The Crown Jewels, London

The Coronation Regalia, to give the Crown Jewels their official name, have been kept in the Tower of London since the 17th century. They are one of the UK's most popular tourist attractions, with around 3 million visitors per year.

Don't miss Cullinan I, the world's largest top-quality cut diamond at 530.2 carats, or the Imperial State Crown, which the monarch wears at the opening of parliament. The Imperial State Crown contains a staggering 2868 diamonds, 17 sapphires, 11 emeralds, 269 pearls and 4 rubies, though the famous 'Black Prince's Ruby' is actually a spinel.

The Victoria and Albert Museum, London

Also in London, the world-famous museum of decorative arts and design, the Victoria and Albert (V&A), is home to a jewellery collection of over 6000 pieces, making it one of the biggest collections in the world. The collection holds pieces that span the millennia from Ancient Egypt to the present day. You can see jewellery given by Queen Elizabeth the 1st to her courtiers, diamonds worn by Catherine the Great of Russia and an emerald necklace given by Napoleon to his adopted daughter. Best of all, you don't have to pay anything to bask in the glory of this collection, as entry to the V&A is free.

The State Diamond Fund, Moscow

The State Diamond Fund is situated within the Kremlin Museum's extensive collection. Entry is strictly controlled but well worth the wait, as the State Diamond Fund contains some truly amazing pieces, including 10 Faberge eggs, the world's largest sapphire, and the crown worn by Catherine the Great. Don't miss the Orlov Diamond, an enormous Indian rose-cut domed diamond of nearly 190 carats, given to Catherine the Great by her former lover Count Orlov.

The Iranian Crown Jewels, Tehran

The world's largest state-owned collection of jewels on display is housed within the Central Bank of Iran. The dazzling display contains extravagant pieces collected since the 16th century by Iran's rulers, and is so valuable that it acts as a reserve for the country's finances. Among its jaw-dropping exhibits are the Darya-e Noor (Sea of Light) diamond, a 186-carat giant and one of the world's largest cut pink diamonds, and the Shahi Sword which is studded with more than 3000 emeralds, rubies, and diamonds on its handle alone. Perhaps most impressive is the 19th century jewel-encrusted globe, commissioned as a way of keeping together the royal treasury's loose gemstones. The globe contains over 51,000 gemstones set in pure gold, with the world's seas and oceans represented by emeralds and the land by rubies and diamonds.

Imperial Treasury, Vienna

If you're ever in Austria, you shouldn't miss this incredible collection of gemstones and jewellery. Located in the 13th century Hofberg Palace, the exhibitions include the world's largest agate bowl

Kim Rix GG (GIA)

(once believed to be the Holy Grail), one of the world's largest emeralds and the imperial regalia of the Holy Roman Empire.

The Smithsonian Natural History Museum, Washington DC

As a museum of natural history, the Smithsonian focuses on gemstones set within its National Gem and Mineral collection, rather than their jewellery setting. It's not as large a collection as some of the other museums I've mentioned, but as it contains what is considered to be the most famous diamond in the world, I couldn't leave it out. The Hope Diamond, a rare deep-blue diamond weighing 45.52 carats, is notorious for bringing bad luck after its theft from an Indian temple — or so the legend goes! It originally weighed a whopping 112 carats, but has been cut and recut in the years since.

Gold Museum (Museo del Oro), Bogotá

It's not hard to understand why the Gold Museum is one of Colombia's most visited tourist attractions. This, the world's largest collection of gold artefacts, contains thousands upon thousands of dazzling gold pieces laid out over three floors. The exhibits include religious offerings, ritual objects and jewellery from the country's pre-Hispanic civilisations. You can also see the museum's collection of raw emeralds, some weighing several kilograms each. All exhibits are accompanied by descriptions in both Spanish and English.

Take advantage of the free tours that run twice a day, or hire an audio guide to get the most out of this journey through Colombia's history.

Slavery tower in the Valle de los Ingenios near Trinidad, Cuba © Kim Rix

Kim Rix GG (GIA)

BRINGING YOUR GEMSTONE
BACK HOME

Queuing outside the VAT Tourist Refund Office, Bangkok Airport, Thailand
© Kim Rix

Kim Rix GG (GIA)

Tax and duty on gemstones

I always recommend that people wear their precious gemstones and jewellery when travelling, as it's far safer to have it on your person than in a handbag or — far worse — in your hold luggage. Most insurance policies will not cover valuables if you let them out of your sight.

Going through UK customs

When going through customs, some people 'forget' to declare their holiday purchases to avoid paying import duty on non-EU overseas goods worth more than the current UK duty-free allowance of £390. If you're tempted to do this, it's worth noting that, besides breaking the law and risking fines or confiscation, you may well be invalidating your insurance should anything happen to your jewellery or gemstones in the future. Many insurance companies will ask to see a copy of the customs declaration for claims on goods bought abroad.

If you would like more information on UK customs duties, visit www.gov.uk/duty-free-goods/declaring-goods

Sending your goods home via post or courier

Perhaps your design won't be ready before it's time to go home. If you choose to have your non-EU holiday purchases delivered to your UK address from abroad, you need to be aware that the charges and allowances for posted items differ from those incurred when bringing your purchases over the UK border in person. You will almost certainly need to pay VAT, and will possibly be charged both VAT *and* import duty:

- VAT is charged on goods worth more than £15 (the allowance for gifts is £39)

- Import duty is charged on goods worth more than £135

Countries other than the UK

Import and tax rules vary from country to country, so if you are taking your gemstone and jewellery purchases home to any country other than the UK, you will need to double check its government website to ensure you are acting within the law.

Tax refunds

When you buy goods abroad, it is likely that the price you pay for many items will include some sort of tax. In the UK this tax is called VAT (value added tax), but it goes by different names in different countries. To encourage tourist spending, many countries allow tourists to reclaim some or all of this tax before leaving the country, usually at the airport. It is certainly worth checking!

If the country you are visiting does offer a tourist tax refund, make sure to do the following:

- Check the rules on what you can claim
- Keep all your receipts
- Allow enough time at the airport — tax refund queues can be very long!

Unusual souvenirs and the law

Rules on what you may take home with you will vary from country to country and you should always check before you attempt to cross the border. In Sri Lanka, for example, you are forbidden from taking rough (uncut) gemstones out of the country. Country-specific details can be found in my *Gemstone Detective* guides relating to each country in the series.

Shopping for the perfect memento of your holiday can present you with some intriguing choices. From locally crafted artefacts to cultural antiques, you may well be attracted to something unlike anything you've ever seen before. As well as being a wonderful reminder of your holiday, it might make a great conversation starter and look beautiful hung up on your wall. That's all well and good, but when buying souvenirs please be mindful, not only of the law but also of the ethical impact of your choices. This is especially important when considering items manufactured from the skins, shells, horns or other parts of endangered animals.

For example, the import of ivory is illegal in the UK and several other countries. The only ivory allowed in is 'antique' (pre-1947) or fossil ivory carrying an authenticating document. Likewise, the UK and several other countries have banned the import of tortoiseshell. Again, you may be allowed to bring such goods through if the tortoiseshell is antique and you have an authenticating document to show at customs.

The most commonly confiscated items at UK customs are:

- Queen Conch shells
- Coral (live or products such as necklaces, earrings and ornaments)
- Turtles & tortoiseshell
- Elephant ivory and skin products

It is always a good idea to check the import rules for your country. If you are caught out, your souvenir will be confiscated, and you may end up with a large fine on top of the wasted purchase cost.

For further guidance, visit: https://www.gov.uk/guidance/cites-controls-import-and-export-of-protected-species

Pink flamingoes, Bahamas © *Kim Rix*

Kim Rix GG (GIA)

The old city of Dubrovnik, Croatia © Kim Rix

Kim Rix GG (GIA)

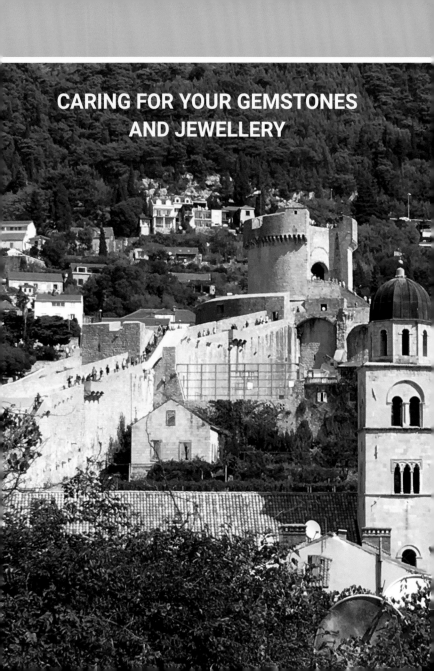

CARING FOR YOUR GEMSTONES
AND JEWELLERY

Musicians in Cuba © Kim Rix

Kim Rix GG (GIA)

How durable is your gemstone?

You'll have noticed that the words 'hard' and 'durable' come up when talking about gemstones. Durability is an umbrella term that encompasses three different aspects of a gemstone's overall toughness.

Hardness

A gemstone's resistance to *scratches*. It is measured using the Mohs scale of hardness, with 1 being very soft and 10 being extremely hard. Talc measures 1 on the Mohs scale, whereas diamond measures 10. One mineral can scratch another if the latter is lower or equal to it on the Mohs scale — for example, the only thing that can scratch a diamond is another diamond. The Mohs scale isn't linear, so diamond, which measures 10, is many times harder than ruby and sapphire at 9.

Toughness

A gemstone's resistance to *chipping, shattering* and *cracking*. Some gems are somewhat brittle, despite being very hard. Rubies and sapphires, for instance, are very resistant to everyday scratches, but can chip if given a hard knock.

Stability

A gemstone's resistance to *change* under different conditions. Some gemstones are sensitive to chemicals, light, heat or humidity levels. Opal, for example, has a high water content and can crack if kept in conditions that are too dry.

Wearing your gemstones and jewellery

It goes without saying that you should not wear soft gemstones for everyday chores! Even hard stones like diamonds, rubies and sapphires can quickly become dull if you do not remove them while washing up, cleaning or gardening.

I always place my rings in a small pot before showering or doing chores. If you make this a habit, you're less likely to misplace your jewellery or lose it altogether.

If your piece of jewellery has pearls in it, it's important to be aware how time and use changes their colour. After a while, pearls will darken slightly as they absorb oils from your skin. Some people see this as a positive change — a way of making your pearl necklace unique to you! However, if you wish to keep your pearls as you bought them, wear them on top of your clothes.

Storing your gemstones and jewellery
Always store your gemstone jewellery in a box appropriate to the piece. The box in which your jewellery was sold is usually fine. Leaving your jewellery out will attract dust and can lead to coloured stones fading in the sunlight. If you would like to streamline your space, make sure you invest in storage designed for the purpose.

Gemstones have different levels of hardness, so some can damage others. Each piece of jewellery needs to have a separate compartment, with enough room for necklaces and bracelets to be fully laid out. This way you'll avoid your favourite jewellery becoming tangled and scratched.

Make sure you lay your pearl necklaces flat to store them. If you hang them up, the silk thread will stretch over time.

Pearl farming © Lauriane Pinsault

Some stones need to be stored in the right conditions. Emerald, opal and pearl benefit from a room that is not too dry.

Cleaning your gemstones and jewellery

When it comes to cleaning your jewellery, it is vital that you know exactly what each gemstone is and what treatment it has undergone. Some gemstones can be irreparably damaged by harsh cleaning agents. If you take your ruby or sapphire to a jeweller to be cleaned and the gem turns out to be a composite stone, the cleaning agent will eat into the glass and destroy the look of your jewellery.

Diamonds, sapphires and rubies are hard enough to be cleaned at home. To do this, mix distilled water with some mild soap and use a soft toothbrush to gently remove dirt. Don't forget to clean underneath the gem as well as on top — when the bottom facets accumulate dirt and grease, your gem won't reflect light as well and will appear dull. Dry and polish your gem with a soft, lint-free cloth to prevent water stains.

Many stones are porous and can be damaged even by water. You should take stones such as opals or emeralds to a professional to be cleaned.

Ultrasonic cleaners

It is always safer to avoid putting your gemstone in an ultrasonic cleaner. Ultrasonic cleaners use high pressure waves to agitate liquid, thus inducing microscopic bubbles which burst against dirt particles and blast them away. While this is great for cleaning silver and gold, it can damage many gemstones beyond repair. Some gemstones are too soft or unstable to stand up to the action of the bubbles and chemical cleaner. Even very hard gemstones like diamond, ruby or sapphire can be damaged if the stone has any miniscule flaws, or if it has been treated in any way.

The following is a list of gemstones you should NEVER put in an ultrasonic cleaner:

- Amber
- Emerald
- Iolite
- Lapis lazuli
- Moonstone
- Onyx
- Opal
- Pearl
- Peridot
- Tanzanite
- Topaz
- Turquoise
- Zircon

Sapphire-covered Virgin Mary, Chanthaburi Cathedral, Thailand © Kim Rix

Top 10 Jewellery Care Tips

1. Take your jewellery off at night, before you get into the shower, start gardening or clean the house. Dirt, chemicals and rough treatment can damage your gemstone and its setting.

2. Don't wear your jewellery in the swimming pool — chlorine corrodes metal and can damage some gemstones.

3. Use only soft, 100% cotton polishing cloths to polish your jewellery or you run the risk of scratching the metal over time. Soft stones should be rinsed in warm water before polishing, to remove any dust particles of hard material that might scratch the stone.

4. Use ultrasonic cleaners with caution. Always check before you clean!

5. Many coloured stones need to be kept away from sunlight to prevent them fading over time. It's never advisable to leave your jewellery in a pool of sunshine! Brown topaz and kunzite are particularly sensitive to fading, whereas amber can become brittle.

Kim Rix GG (GIA)

6. Never store silver in a damp environment, as it will tarnish quickly.

7. Unlike silver, pearls and opals like moisture. It's good to store them in a damp environment like the bathroom.

8. Make sure to store your pearl necklaces flat, to prevent the silk stretching.

9. Gold used for rings should not be more than 18 carat gold otherwise the metal will be too soft to withstand the little knocks that are part of everyday life.

10. Give jewellery as a gift and to celebrate important milestones in your life. Every time the piece is worn, it will act as a special reminder of that occasion.

Repairs
If your gemstone becomes dull, your setting loose or you need to have a ring resized, you should always take it to an expert.

It's important that you let your jeweller know about any treatment your gemstone has had. Some treatments can disguise vulnerabilities in your gemstone that make it more prone to damage from cleaning or repairs.

Looking out over the old city of Kotor, Montenegro © *Kim Rix*

Kim Rix GG (GIA)

Machu Picchu, Peru © Kim Rix

Kim Rix GG (GIA)

APPENDICES

Mediterranean © Kim Rix

Kim Rix GG (GIA)

Glossary

Adularescence An optical effect that makes a gemstone appear to glow from within. Moonstones exhibit adularescence.

Asterism An optical effect in which a six-rayed star appears to float just beneath the surface of the gem. Gemstones exhibiting asterism are given the name 'star'.

Bi colour A gemstone that contains two different colours.

Brilliance The 'flashing' effect produced by light entering the stone and bouncing off its interior facets. Only transparent stones can be said to have brilliance.

Cabochon The most common form of gem cutting, in which the stone is cut with a flat bottom and a rounded top or 'high-domed' face in cut opal.

Carats A carat is a metric unit of weight used to measure the size of all finished faceted gemstones. Carat is also the term used to measure the purity of gold. Pure gold is 24 carat.

Certificate Confirmation that the gem in question is authentic.

Chatoyancy An optical effect in which a straight line appears to float just beneath the surface of the gem. Gemstones exhibiting chatoyancy are called 'cat's eye' stones.

Clarity Relates to the types of inclusions (flaws) in a gemstone.

Colour change   A gemstone that appears to be different colours in different light conditions.

Corundum   A very hard, transparent mineral. Ruby and sapphire are colour variations of corundum.

Cutting   The process of shaping and polishing a rough stone.

Durability   A gemstone's resistance to scratching, chipping, shattering, cracking and structural change.

Faceting   Cutting.

Fire   The tendency of a stone's structure to split white light into the colours of the rainbow. Diamond is famous for this.

Flash   The effect caused by light diffraction on the internal structure of an opal.

Grading report   A detailed analysis of a gemstone's quality.

Heat treatment   A traditional method of improving the clarity of a gemstone. Not all gems can be treated in this way, but almost all sapphires are.

Hue   The colour of a stone.

Imitation   A stone that imitates a more expensive stone. An imitation stone might be a less valuable semi-precious stone, or it might simply be coloured glass. Or it might simply be coloured glass that resembles something much more valuable.

Inclusion   A fleck of material within a stone; a flaw.

Iridescence   The display of rainbow colours on the surface of the stone as the viewing angle changes.

Jargoon   An old name for zircon that still crops up here and there.

Loupe   A small magnifying glass used to examine gems.

Lustre   The 'gleam' produced by light bouncing off the surface of a stone.

Mohs scale   A system that grades minerals from softest to hardest on a scale of 1-10. Talc is the softest material at 1, whereas diamond is the hardest at 10. A mineral can only be scratched by a mineral equal or harder than it on the Mohs scale.

Padparadscha   A specific and rare variety of sapphire, with an unusual orangey-pink hue.

Pleochroic   The display of different colours from different directions.

Refractive index   A measure of the change in the speed and angle of light as it passes through a material.

Rough stone   A natural gemstone before it has been cut, or 'faceted'.

Saturation   The intensity of colour in a gemstone.

Synthetic   A gemstone identical in structure to a mined gemstone, but formed in a lab rather than naturally in the earth.

Tone   How light or dark a gemstone appears to be.

Window   An area within a gemstone that does not reflect light and therefore appears flat and dull. It's called a window because you can see through it.

Chichen Itza, Mexico © Kim Rix

Kim Rix GG (GIA)

Birthstones and Anniversary stones

Birthstones by month:

Month		Stone
January		Garnet
February		Amethyst
March		Aquamarine
April		Diamond
May		Emerald
June		Alexandrite or pearl
July		Ruby
August		Peridot
September		Sapphire
October		Tourmaline or opal
November		Topaz or citrine
December		Turquoise, tanzanite or zircon

Birthstones by day:

Day	Colour	Gem
Sunday	Red	Ruby
Monday	Yellow/cream	Yellow sapphire, diamond or pearl
Tuesday	Pink	Pink sapphire or tourmaline
Wednesday	Green	Emerald, green sapphire or green jade
Thursday	Orange/brown	Cat's eye chrysoberyl, orange garnet or orange sapphire
Friday	Light blue	Blue sapphire
Saturday	Purple	Amethyst, violet spinel or purple sapphire

Gold Souk in Dubai, UAE © Kim Rix

Kim Rix GG (GIA)

Gemstone Wedding Anniversaries:

2nd		Garnet
3rd		Pearl
5th		Sapphire
6th		Amethyst
10th		Diamond
11th		Turquoise
14th		Opal
15th		Ruby
16th		Peridot
19th		Aquamarine
20th		Emerald
23rd		Topaz
30th		Pearl
35th		Emerald
40th		Ruby
45th		Sapphire
60th		Diamond

The Navaratna

On a visit to south-east Asia, you will almost certainly come across the term 'Navaratna' — a Sanskrit word meaning 'nine gems.' Navaratna is a piece of jewellery set with a combination of nine gemstones, which ancient astrology connects with nine astronomical bodies.

Though the origins of Navaratna jewellery are uncertain, the association of gemstones with the stars, moons and planets is found in ancient Hindu texts. The Navaratna has cultural significance across India and south-east Asia, where its gems are believed to harness the positive characteristics and ward off the negative energies of the nine major celestial bodies in Hindu astrology. Belief in the power of the Navaratna is common to many religions, including Hinduism, Buddhism, Jainism and Sikhism.

The Navaratna ring, Myanmar (Burma) © Kim Rix

Kim Rix GG (GIA)

Astrologists believe that the position of the stars and planets at our birth affects the course of our life. Because of this, the arrangement of the gemstones in each piece of Navaratna jewellery is significant. Ruby, which represents the sun, tends to be found at the centre of the arrangement. Many people who wear the Navaratna will consult an astrologer before having the stones set in an arrangement that is considered particularly lucky for them. The order in which the stones are set is also considered important. Often the birthstone is the first to be incorporated into its jewellery setting.

Traditionally, gems used in the Navaratna should have good clarity. Gemstones that are cracked or significantly flawed are thought to block the passage of light through the gemstones and so weaken — or even reverse — their positive effects.

The gemstones of the Navaratna can vary depending on the country.

Sandy beach, Cayo Coco, Cuba © Kim Rix

Holiday reading

If you would like to take your interest in gemstones further, the GIA offer a recommended reading list:
https://www.gia.edu/library-recommended-books-gemology

As a gemmologist, I have a library of gem-related books. My favourite book for reference is:

Secrets of the Gem Trade: The Connoisseur's Guide to Precious Gemstones by Richard W. Wise

I also have collected many books about opals, written by Len Cram

Another good book is *Gemstones – Understanding, Identifying, Buying* – by Keith Wallis FGA

Other resources

The GIA has 10 locations around the world and offers a range of courses including Distance Education – a combination of two online eLearning courses and one hands-on lab class. Lab classes are offered at GIA campuses worldwide.

For a list of their locations, visit www.gia.edu/locations

The Gemmological Association of Great Britain (Gem-A).
Gem-A offers a range of short courses, workshops and lab classes:
www.gem-a.com/about/find-us

There is a huge array of ways to learn for free on the internet:
https://beyond4cs.com/free-gemology-courses-and-resources/

Acknowledgements

The following people have helped immeasurably in my quest for the knowledge I am sharing in these pages. Their warm hospitality, true friendship and incredible generosity have made this book possible. I owe them a huge debt of thanks!

Justin K Prim, Simon Dussart, Billie Hughes, Vincent Pardieu, Ony CH, Kae Napaporn, Manura Ekanayake , Ni-Ransha Fernando, Affi Zubair, Nashan Mohamed, Shaminda Aakarsha, Mohamed Althad Suhar, Danuna Tillakaratne, Manju Kumara, Adnan Akber Cassim, Akber Cassim, Janaka Abayawickram, Farhan Fyzee, Cindy Kelly, Daryl Bonham, Rata Jackson, Len Cram, Alison Summerville, Peter Shermam, Mr Richardson, Shortie, Sandra de Jong, Lorraine & Peter Coulton, Elaine Raines, Sue White, Sally Patel, Naing Family, Feroze Dada FCA, CTA, Brig General Tin Maung Swe, U Khin Maung, Mee Nge, Stuart Pool, Marcus Mccallum FGA, Ronnie Bauer, Cathryn Hillcoat, Adam McIntosh and Jan Calligan.

A very special thanks to the friends and family who have helped me bring this book to publication.

Fiona Crehan, Judeline Nicholas, Valerie McKie, Sheila Aly, Sarada Chaudhuri, Helen Turier, Judith Katz, May Swan-Easton.

Of course, thanks must go to everyone at Filament Publishing for their efficiency and professionalism in bringing this latest book to the wider world. Also thanks to Clare and Emma at Fusion3media for their creative input and teamwork.

Finally, I take this opportunity to thank my husband, Steven, for his steadfast support through my many and long absences in the course of researching this series.

About the author

Kim Rix is a professional photographer, gemmologist (GIA) and the author of the *Gemstone Detective* series. She travels extensively and has gathered a vast amount of the best local knowledge from her worldwide contacts.

Buying Gemstones and Jewellery Worldwide is the fourth in Kim's *Gemstone Detective* series. Groups interested in arranging speaking engagements may contact her via her website or email her directly at kim@gemstonedetective.com.

Disclaimer: Kim Rix travels for research purposes and to gain insight into the marketplace with the intention of writing the *Gemstone Detective* series of books. Any resulting articles or publications should not be taken or used as an endorsement.

If I have made any errors in this book, please

 Forgive me

 Correct me

 Contact: kim@gemstonedetective.com

Kim Rix GG (GIA)

Connect with Kim

Kim would love you to review the book on Amazon and share your experiences with her on any of these social media platforms:

 www.facebook.com/GemstoneDetective

 www.twitter.com/kimrix

 www.instagram.com/gemstone_detective

You can also sign up to receive Kim's latest news and travels straight to your inbox via her website:

 www.gemstonedetective.com

Next books...

This series began in 2018 with *Buying Gemstones and Jewellery in Sri Lanka*. Look out for my upcoming *Gemstone Detective* books before you shop in the following countries:

- Australia   to be published on 22 January, 2019
- Thailand   to be published on 22 January, 2019
- India   to be published on 14 May, 2019
- USA   to be published on 26 November, 2019
- Brazil
- Namibia
- South Africa
- Tanzania
- Vietnam
- Myanmar
- Canada